MW01058762

Writings of Big Bill Haywood

Speeches and Pamphlets on Unions, Socialism, Syndicalism, and Revolution

William Haywood

Red and Black Publishers, St Petersburg, Florida

Industrial Socialism published 1911 by Charles Kerr Co., Chicago

Library of Congress Cataloging-in-Publication Data

Haywood, Big Bill, 1869-1928.
    Writings of Big Bill Haywood : speeches and pamphlets on unions, socialism, syndicalism, and revolution / William Haywood.
       p. cm.
    ISBN 978-1-61001-010-8
1. Working class--United States--History. 2. Labor unions--United States--History. 3. Socialism--United States--History. I. Title.
    HD8072.H33 2011
    331.88'6092--dc22

                                                      2011000020

Red and Black Publishers, PO Box 7542, St Petersburg, Florida, 33734
Contact us at: info@RedandBlackPublishers.com
          Printed and manufactured in the United States of America

Contents

Industrial Socialism

by William D. Haywood And Frank Bohn

Foreword

Socialism is the future system of industrial society. Toward it America, Europe, Australasia, South Africa and Japan are rapidly moving. Under capitalism today the machines and other means of wealth production are privately owned. Under Socialism tomorrow they will be collectively owned. Under capitalism all popular constitutional government is merely political. Its main purpose is the protection of private property. Industry is at present governed by a few tyrants. Its purpose is to give to the workers as little wealth as possible. Under Socialism industrial government will be more democratic than political government is today. Its purpose will be to manage production and to establish and conduct the great social institutions required by civilized humanity. Political government will then, of course, have ceased to exist.

This booklet is primarily an introduction to the study of Socialism. Its title has been chosen advisedly. But the authors have also in mind a second purpose. While there have been published a number of booklets with the contents of which they are in entire agreement, none has yet appeared in English which attempts to cover the whole matter of Socialist principles and tactics from the industrial standpoint. The point of view of industrial unionism is to them the most essential factor in the study of Socialism. Without that the whole literature of economics, politics and history is entirely worthless to the working class. With it the Socialist education of the workers begins. The authors are constantly presenting this point of view from the rostrum. This booklet makes it accessible to all those who wish to understand it.

I— Industrial Slavery

The Most Wonderful Thing in the World

The most wonderful thing in the world today is not at all "grand", "beautiful," or "inspiring." It is the most terrible as well as the most wonderful thing in the world. At first it excites only fear and horror. We do not here mean some frightful earthquake, nor plague of disease, nor war. The most wonderful and terrible fact in the world is the present condition of the working class.

In the United States 30,000,000 people work for other people, to whom they yield more than two-thirds of their product for the privilege of working.

These working people have usually nothing at all to say as regards the amount they receive, the conditions of their labor and when they shall be at work and when at leisure. They are permitted to live in this country only so long as the few capitalists in it give them work and thus permit them to stay.

The working people of the United States produce more wealth in one year than was ever produced in any other nation in the same period in the world's history. But these workers are becoming thinner, shorter, weaker — that is, they have less life — than the American people of fifty years ago.

In the United States 750,000 workers are killed and wounded in the shops and mines and on the railroads every year.

The vast majority of the toilers in the United States die premature deaths of diseases caused by overwork, by underfeeding and diseases caused by dirt — dirt in the air, dirt in the drinking water, dirt and poison in the workers' food.

The idle rich of the United States waste more wealth than any other idle rich class have wasted in the history of the world. One woman spends $127,000 a year for "clothing." Dogs which cost $10,000 or $15,000 are now fashionable as pets among the rich. The idle rich of the United States import annually nearly $40,000,000 worth of precious stones. Many of them have, beside a great mansion in New York, Chicago, San Francisco, and one or more large country estates here, a town house in Paris or London, and a country estate or two in England or France. For all this they produce nothing. Their time is occupied spending the millions others have produced.

The great wealth of the United States has been created by its toilers alone. It is being wasted by its idlers. The working people are sweating, starving and dying.

The most wonderful thing in the world is the fact that this great working class of the United States, 30,000,000 strong, should so peaceably and quietly go on in the same old way.

The Life Of The Worker

The average wage earner of today is born of poor parents who work for a living. These may be "well paid" or "poorly paid." That is, the father may receive $5.00 a day and keep his family in a comfortable cottage. He may receive only $1.75 per day and be often out of a job. Then the mother and the older children must work in order to get enough for the family to live upon. In either case, sooner or later, the children of the wage worker hunt for jobs of their own.

When the worker gets his first job the world about him takes off its mask. He sees it as it is. Hours are long and most work is monotonous. Any child or young person naturally very much dislikes this first harsh experience of the world of the working class. His games and fun-making are given up. His physical growth is stunted and his mind dwarfed more or less. Long ago nearly all of the young men who went to work for wages began by learning a trade. This trade was very often extremely interesting to them. It educated their minds and developed their bodies. If they were apprenticed at eighteen, then, perhaps at twenty-one, they were sure of steady work and good wages. Today very few of the working people learn a trade. They work in some factory, store or office at tasks which they perform as well in a month as they do in ten years. If the young wage earner is vigorous in mind and body he revolts at this labor and makes a desperate struggle to secure an education or otherwise make it possible for himself to rise out of the working class. The stronger and healthier his body and the keener his mind, the harder does he fight. But he finds, except in very rare instances, that the doors of opportunity are closed to the children of the workers.

If the young worker learns one of the trades which still remain in modern industry, he finds after he has learned it that it also is being abolished by the invention of new machinery. He may go to night school and complete a course of study, or take a correspondence course in mechanics or some other form of applied science. If he does he will discover that his knowledge, gotten at such sacrifice of time, savings and effort, will not raise his wages. There are now so many educated poor people that their pay is on the average much less than that of skilled workers in the trades. Another hope of the young workers, men and women, is to save money and start in some small business. Others have risen and become wealthy. Why not they? So, by giving up all pleasures, by overwork and pitiful economies, does the young worker make his start in business. If he has been fortunate enough not to lose his money through some bank swindle, he at last, after years of effort, tries his luck. The best data we have show that more than nine-tenths of those who engage in small business fail utterly. The small portion who "succeed" do so by working night and day, Sundays and holidays. Even they make but meager livings, no better on the average than the wage-workers.

The hearts and minds of nearly all young American working people are full of hope. They cannot conceive that it could be possible for them to toil on throughout their lifetime for small wages and every day find the work getting harder. They do not at first realize what it is to be a wage-worker. They are unmarried and hence often have a little more money than is absolutely necessary to keep them. This the young workers usually spend for good clothes and for an occasional holiday, The daily grind of labor has not yet deadened their minds nor crushed their spirits. Plans for advancement are constantly being formed.

Then come marriage and responsibility for a family. Perhaps the care of aged parents adds to the burden. In any case by the time the worker is twenty-five years of age he has lost his grip on his hope for something better. At thirty, with growing burdens, he gets to be quite content to work along day by day without looking forward to anything but his Saturday pay envelope. He is likely to be afflicted by some chronic illness due to the nature of his work or the insanitary condition of his factory or home. Perhaps illness in his family, or the birth of a number of children, so increase his burden that his struggle becomes a pitiless daily conflict to live.

At thirty-five years of age these conditions, coupled with occasional unemployment, drive the worker often to despair. But later he gets used to it. Poor food, shoddy clothing, a shack to live in, unemployment—these are his lot in life and he makes the best of it. The old saying of the poet, "Hope springs eternal in the human breast," is not at all true of the working people of today. In them hope dies. At forty or fifty years of age the average worker plods along rather carelessly. If he suffers an injury in the factory he eats without worry the bread of charity, which, twenty years before, he would have despised. He knows that he cannot educate his children. He may see them go early to work and injure their health. But he is so happy to receive their weekly wage to help out at home that he forgets that they are young and should be at play or at school.

This man is exactly what the owners and rulers of America now wish him to be. He is strong enough to do the work they want done. He does not demand vacations and amusement, a better home and education for his children. So he will not strike for more wages. The vast majority of the American working people over forty years of age cannot be made to understand their condition. Life for them has lost all light and beauty and hence all desire for more of its good things. Quite as hopeless is the state of mind of some of the younger workers. A portion of these, born of parents broken and weary from work, and themselves underfed and sent early to factories, are as careless about their conditions of life as are their parents. But with a majority of the young and a considerable minority of the older folks this is not true. They want more wages and less work. They desire rest and leisure, a chance to know their family and friends better, and an occasional vacation in the country. They wish to read, hear good music and go to theaters. Above all they crave better food and more of it and they know that their limbs are stiff because of the lack of enough rest and exercise.

To such, and such only, are the following pages addressed. Those who are utterly broken in body and decayed in mind, those who are deadened beyond being moved by the facts of life, those who think that they somehow deserve all the labor and pain and misery of the world and that a few others should enjoy plenty and peace and opportunity, we earnestly request to at once pass this booklet along to someone else. For it can be of no interest to themselves.

We see today a working class bowed down by labor. We see it starved by poverty. We see all its efforts to improve its condition met by blows in the face. We see babies dying because their parents cannot support them. We see tender children enslaved in mines and sweatshops. We see strong men committing crimes because they cannot find masters. We see the aged, after lives of long and loving service, begging for bread and craving death.

Socialism is a message of hope. It is addressed to the working class. It will save the working class, or rather, show the working class how to save itself. The world does not need to be cursed by long labor, by low wages, by starvation, by worry, and by disease. Millions now know that these conditions may be completely changed. When enough of the workers understand Socialism, believe in it, and are firmly resolved to have it, the time will be ripe for the change. That change is coming. It is coming soon. Every added recruit who will read and think brings it nearer.

"On we march then, we the workers, and the rumor that ye hear
   Is the blended sound of battle and deliverance drawing near;
   For the hope of every creature is the banner that we bear,
   And the world is marching on."

II — Industrial Progress

The Private Property Superstition.

The working class is today enslaved chiefly because it does not understand the conditions of its life and labor. A few rich people own the lands and machines. The many labor and have nothing. This every worker knows. But why is this so? How long has it been thus? How long is it likely to continue? And most important of all, what are the workers going to do in order to help themselves? When we ask these questions, we find that very few workers can give a clear and satisfactory answer. Only when they can answer these questions will the first great step toward a better condition have been taken.

The Story of the Island.

Let us simplify the problem. Imagine that instead of continuing to work here in America among the 30,000,000 workers on this great continent, ten workers should go off to an uninhabited tropical island which is only ten square miles in area. There they would not need expensive houses and clothing, nor would they have to lay by great supplies of food for the winter. A very small amount of labor would be enough to support a family. Now let us suppose that when the ten went ashore on that island, one of their number should step forward and say:

"This is my island. I hold here a document which proves it. This document was received by my great-great-grandfather from the King of Great Britain in 1760. Of course the King never saw the island, neither did my great-great-grandfather. But I am his only living heir. So the island is all mine. The law permits me to do with it what I wish. I am not going to drive you away. In fact, I shall not stay myself unless you do. I see that you have tools with which to cultivate the soil. Go to work at once. I shall charge you for rent only three-fourths of what you produce. That is, if any of you produce a hundred bushels of sweet potatoes, I shall take seventy-five and leave you twenty-five. Each of you will need all that is left you, but of course I shall not need all that I receive. I shall be paid as rent twenty-seven times as much as any of you are permitted to keep. I shall use of this one part, and send twenty-six parts to America. There it will be sold and for the money I shall buy machines. When the machines come you need no longer pay me rent. Each of you will then produce 1,000 bushels. Instead of letting you keep twenty-five bushels, as I did when you rented the land of me, I shall pay you only enough money to buy back fifteen bushels. If you do not wish to work for me you need not. You will still be free citizens of this island. Those who think I am not leaving them enough may stop working. There is the sea. You may jump into it. In that case I can get plenty others from the cities of the United States who will gladly come here and take your places. I shall, however, at once make one of you a policeman, who will club the remainder of you and imprison you if you get to be unruly and disobey the laws I make. I shall very soon bring a lawyer here. He will teach you to respect this holy document I hold in my hand. It is the foundation of our property and of our liberties. The first task to be performed is to build me a mansion on the hill. After that, if there be any timber left, you may build yourself some shacks here on the beach."

So situated, the propertyless workers would quickly understand their condition. Unless they were bereft of reason by respect for the property rights of the individual, they would simply laugh at the document and its owner. They would probably go to work for themselves, each taking his whole product and leaving the "owner" only what he himself produced.

North America No Different.

The working people of North America are in much the same condition as the nine workers on the island would have been had they quietly consented to become enslaved. But the island was very small and North America is very great. The island had ten people, North America has more than 100,000,000. On the island there was but one old worm-eaten paper which established the owner's right to property in the land. In North America the workers behold a great mass of laws, old and new, which they have been carefully taught to respect and obey. These laws were made by the political and legal servants of the masters. They were created for the purpose of protecting property which existed long before the law gave the owners a "right" to it. Yet all the rights which the capitalists claim are based on these laws. As soon as the workers determine to abolish them, or ignore them, the capitalist's "right" to what the workers have produced will cease to exist.

If this seems very strange and hard to understand it is because of the great area and population of America and the long time it has taken to create the present gigantic system of industry with its protecting laws and government. So the first matter to deal with and understand is the nature of this system of industry.

The Growth Of The Machine Process

How have our mines and factories and railroads come to be just what they are? There was a time in America when every young man could start out and make a living for himself without begging work from someone who had it to offer. The cobbler owned his shop and small tools. The carpenter built the cobbler's shop and the cobbler mended the carpenter's shoes. This was a fair exchange of labor. No one was robbed. How different it is today. The shoe workers in some of our large factories make on the average twelve pairs of shoes for each worker in a day, but they get only the price of one, or less, as wages. The carpenters build mansions for the rich and live in miserable tenements, which are also owned by those same rich. How did all this come about?

From Hand Labor to Machine Labor.

The story of the past is one long tale of constant changes in human labor and human life. More of these changes occurred in the nineteenth century than in any other century in human existence. Greater changes occurred in America during this century than in any other country. In America they were, in fact, so great and far-reaching in their effects that the coming change to Socialism will not be, in itself, nearly so wonderful. To begin with, in 1790 the population of the United States numbered less than 4,000,000. Nearly all these people lived on a narrow strip of land along the Atlantic coast. In 1910 the population had spread over the whole continent. In this short period of time North America was won from the wilderness and turned into a nation of farms, factories and railroads. It was surely a greater task for the American working people to conquer the wilderness than it will be for their descendants of the twentieth century to reconquer America from the few capitalists who have taken it from them. But this great change brought about by the workers of the last century could not have taken place had it not been for a change in the methods of work which everywhere came with it. We refer to the change from hand labor to machine labor.

This was the most important revolution that the world has ever known. We must relate briefly how it took place in America. For unless it is understood, Socialism and the Socialist Movement cannot be understood.

Cloth-Making.

Before the year 1800 most of the cloth worn in America was spun and woven in the homes of the people. A farmer would own a few sheep and himself clip their wool. His wife and daughters then took this wool, cleaned, spun and carded it, and wove it into cloth. Of the cloth they made clothing for all the members of the family. Thus no capitalist was permitted to take a large part of their product for permitting them to work.

Two machines brought about a great change in this important work. The first was the spinning machine, which was invented in England in 1764. A weaver named Hargreaves, who could neither read nor write, got the idea and successfully worked it out. It was one of the most important inventions of all history and therefore Hargreaves was one of the greatest men who ever lived. But the historians have not been much interested in what the working people have done, although they have done almost everything worthwhile in the world.

This machine was improved by others and finally brought to a state of great perfection. The first American factory to use cotton spinning machinery was built in Rhode Island in 1791. These factories would probably have not been very successful in America had it not been for another important machine invented in 1793. This was Whitney's cotton-gin. Like Hargreaves, and nearly all other inventors, Whitney was a poor man, being a school teacher. He died poor. The cotton-gin made it possible to raise cotton over the whole of the Southern states. It was probably the most important machine ever invented in America, as it gave long life to chattel slavery and thus brought about the Civil War. These machines made cotton and cotton cloth cheap. The whole industry of cloth-making was taken from the homes to factories. In 1804 there were only four textile mills in operation. In 1811 there were 87 mills, with 80,000 spindles and 4,000 wage-workers. In 1815 there were 76,000 workers in the textile factories. This development was brought about practically by the War of 1812 and the trouble with Great Britain leading up to it, which kept British goods out of the American market.

Since that time this industry has grown wonderfully. The machines have been constantly improved. At first it took a worker to tend each machine. At the present time much of the cotton and wool is spun and woven almost automatically. In some cases the worker tends twelve machines, the product of these being 300 yards of cloth a day. It was of a great benefit to the capitalists that women and children could operate textile machinery. This made wages low and profits large. And where wages are low and profits are large we have a heaven for the capitalist and a hell for the wage-worker. Hours are usually long—ten hours a day being the rule in the North and twelve hours in the South. In the South tens of thousands of very small children, many under eight years of age, are employed in this industry. In some cases wages are so low that the capitalist takes more in profits every year than his whole plant is worth. A great many kinds of cloth are now made by machines. The workers produce silks and fine woolens for their idle masters. For themselves they buy, with their small wages, cheap cottons and shoddy goods made out of old rags.

Working people invented practically all of the machines. Working people raise all of the cotton and wool. Working people manufacture the cloth. But the idle capitalists own the machines. That is the cause of the great injury done the workers.

Power Machinery.

Who shall do the work? We have already asked and partially answered this question. Generally speaking, people do not work any more than they must. The poor must work or starve. That is why one finds them always so busy. But machines are cheaper to keep than people. That is why machines have been so much introduced by the capitalists. Machines do not have to be fed and clothed. Also, it does not cost so much to make machines as it does to raise children. So the machine process permits the capitalists to pay the worker just enough to keep himself. Low wages, therefore, force the working people to take their children to the factory. Very often the children can secure work when there is none to be had for the parents. He will do the work who will work cheapest.

Wanted, Cheap Power.

Most wage-workers are today occupied in tending machines. That is, they set the machines to work, feed in the raw material, and take away the product. The first machines were run by hand. Hand power or human power has been the oldest and most common form of power. But to the employer this method is very expensive, because he must pay back so large a portion of the worker's product in wages. There have been many forms of power developed to take the place of the strength of the individual worker. These have been, chiefly, the power of animals, of falling water, of the winds, of steam, of electricity, and of ignited fuel gases, such as gasoline. All of these have been of tremendous importance in the history of industry. Without the help of draft animals in agriculture and land transportation, and of the sailing vessel for water transportation, it is doubtful whether civilization could ever have developed. Steam power came to be used about the same time that cloth-making machinery was invented. It was soon applied to the many other machines which were developed in rapid succession. The nineteenth century was the century of the steam engine. In England it was used to operate textile machinery as early as 1779. Even before that time it had been used to pump water out of the coal mines and to bring coal to the surface. This greatly cheapened the production of coal and therefore of iron. Cheap iron made possible cheap steam engines and other machines. So the various industries that were developing helped one another along.

The Steamboat and Locomotive

In America the steamboat was first developed about 1785, but not made profitable until Fulton navigated up the Hudson in 1807. The many excellent streams for water power long kept the stationary steam-engine from coming into use as rapidly in America as in England. In 1829 the first locomotive was operated in the United States. In 1830 there were only twenty-three miles of railroad; in 1840, eighteen hundred miles; in 1850, seven thousand miles; in 1860, thirty thousand miles; in 1870, seventy-two thousand miles. At the present time the United States contains 240,000 miles of railroad. This great growth in the means of transportation, together with the development of the postal system, telegraph and telephone, has developed the national and international market. So long as machines must be run by hand, by horse power or by water power, factories were small and therefore their output was limited. A large number of these small factories could not be located in one place, even if water power could be had, because of the great cost of transportation. Small factories were therefore scattered about the country wherever there was good water power and the markets were near at hand. The brains of a capitalist might have been ever so great, they could not outrun the conditions of industry. The whole nation went forward together, everybody except the idlers among the capitalists helping in the progress. Of course the great inventors did more than anybody else, but a large number would be working at one invention at a time, and many failures were usually required to develop the knowledge which finally made one inventor successful.

So power machinery has grown to its present great proportions. The real difference between the America of today and the America of the Revolutionary War period is the difference between an ox-team hauling a ton and a great locomotive hauling 5,000 tons. The greatest of the modern locomotives thus does the work of 10,000 oxen or horses. In the factories, meanwhile, the stationary steam-engine and the electric dynamo have developed to the same degree. One man working with modern machines is thus able to do the work of one hundred, one thousand or even five thousand men working without machines. But these foolish workers work harder than ever they did before. If they cannot keep up with the machines they are discharged and others hired.

Farming Machinery.

In agriculture the change from small tools to machines has been almost as great as in manufacturing. Nearly all of the work now done on farms is done by machines. It was the second quarter of the nineteenth century that witnessed the great changes on the American farm. McCormick, a farm boy in Virginia, invented the reaper. This made it possible for the Western states to become the greatest grain-producing area in the world. Cheap food meant cheap working people in the cities. So American capitalists were permitted to compete for the world's markets.

For a long time, down even till 1900, farmers who owned one hundred or two hundred acres of land could make good use of the machines which had been invented. Their children could help run the machines and thus they kept all the profits. At most they hired one or two wage-workers, with a few extra during the summer months. But the machine process has now outgrown the size of the old-fashioned farm. Plows are being drawn by traction engines. Grain is being reaped and threshed by great machines which the small farmer cannot afford to buy and could not profitably use even if he possessed them. Above all, science is being applied to farming. The raising of crops, the breeding and care of cattle, and all the other work of the farm must be carefully studied. One man cannot possibly know all that must be known in this great and ever changing industry. So we must have farms of greater and greater area, where work may be specialized and where all the modern machines and scientific methods may be put to good use. This means that very soon only great capitalists can get profits out of a farm. The farm has been the last place where a man with a small amount of money could go to work, be his own boss and make a good living. But soon this will be impossible. In fact, in many states it is already impossible. Whenever the farmer must rent his farm he is no better off than the wage-worker in the city. It is safe to say that half the farmers in America receive no more for their long days of hard work than unskilled day laborers.

Mining.

Before the coming of steam-power, coal mining was of very little importance. Now it is one of the most necessary industries we have. Coal is not only used for steam. It is also the most important domestic fuel in the United States. In the form of coke it is necessary to the manufacture of iron. The United States is now first in the production of coal.

A hundred years ago, when coal mining began in this country, any farmer on whose land there cropped out a vein might open a mine and sell the product. Today the coal-miners work for great trusts. They use machines and other expensive apparatus. The mines which employ the largest number of workers turn out the coal most cheaply. Even if a man with a small tract of coal land could operate a mine successfully, he could not dispose of his product, because the great companies and trusts own the terminals, get better rates from the railroads and have the markets monopolized.

In metal mining great capital is even more strongly intrenched. When gold was first discovered in California, a workingman, if fortunate enough to find a deposit, could wash out the precious metal in a pan. But this method is now a thing of the past. In the West, gold, silver and copper are taken from rock and soil which must be worked by expensive machines. All of the great copper mines of Montana are owned by the Standard Oil interests. The Smelter Trust, under the control of the Guggenheims, has possession of a large part of both the mining and smelter industries. If a man in the West, after a long search, discovers a rich mine, he cannot work it without large capital. If he refuses to sell it for a small sum, one of the great companies will swindle him out of it. All he can then do is to go to work for wages in the mine.

The Making of Iron and Steel.

In this great and important industry we have the best example of industrial progress. A hundred years ago it was conducted like any other small business. One man would own a mine and another would burn charcoal on his farm. These men would sell their product to a third man who owned a forge and made the iron. This raw iron was sold to a man who had a shop for working it. Finally a man with a rolling and slitting mill, who put it into shape for the nail-maker, or the blacksmith.

With every development of new machines for working iron and steel this industry has grown. Thirty years ago there were still a large number of high-paid workers in the iron and steel industries. Strength and skill were required to puddle the molten metal or work it into the finished product. Then came the blast furnace, and finally the Martin-Siemans process of making open-hearth steel. These drove the old-fashioned steel worker to the scrap heap along with the small tools he used. The iron ore now goes into one end of the mill and the finished product comes out of the other. For a man with a few hundred or a few thousand dollars, to start in the iron or steel business would be ridiculous. The great Steel Trust now owns its own extensive mines, lines of railroad, and a fleet of vessels on the Great Lakes. It has a large number of gigantic iron and steel plants which produce from sixty percent to seventy percent of the iron and steel of America. The Trust could, if it thought it wise to do so, crush out all competitors in a year's time.

It is plain even from this short survey of American industries that the day of the small producer is past. Intelligent people always do their work in the easiest and quickest way. The manufacturer who produces his product the most cheaply, survives. Others perish. So those who live and maintain their standing in modern business are such as control the large capital necessary to buy the best and most machines and organize the greatest business.

The Machines Are Here to Stay.

When machines were first invented some very foolish working people attempted to destroy them. It was seen that the machines would take the place of workers and thus do them harm. The workers did not then understand that the time would come when they could join together and own and control the machines and thus be able to work much shorter hours. All they saw was that the machines were doing them harm at the time. But workingmen, either organized or unorganized, can never fight the machines successfully. They must always accept the new machine and learn to work it. Machines are now displacing glass workers of all kinds, plumbers, carpenters and other woodworkers, printers, and, in fact, almost every kind of worker there is. This process will not stop. On the contrary it will go on ever more rapidly. The unemployed army will grow greater and greater. Women and children wage-earners will more and more take the place of men. Already there are at work for wages in America, 4,000,000 children and 7,000,000 women.

There is no chivalry in the workshop. Capitalism compels sex equality. At present it is equality in a common slavery.

Let the Machines Work for the Workers.

One of the worst features about the members of the working class is that they do not think themselves happy unless they are hard at work. Instead of letting the machines do the work many workers would rather do it themselves. This comes from the fact that there was a time when there were very few idlers and when all the workers, both men and women, were forced to toil constantly in order to live. The working class thus got into the habit of work. It now finds it very hard to give up the bad habit, even though only a little work is necessary.

Machines have come to free the working class. Until the invention of machines workers were enslaved by small tools to the soil. For them it was work or starve. Work or starve it is still, not because nature enforces slavery, but because they have not yet seen their way out of it. They are enslaved not to the soil but to the people who own the machines. The Socialist Movement has come to place the machines, the shops, the railroads, the land and the mines in the possession of the workers. That will mean freedom, security and opportunity for all who live.

Ill — Industrial Organization

The Foundations of Government.

The world is ruled by force. The foundation of this force is control over a large number of people. The capitalists rule the world today because they have organized the workers in the shops and control them. They own and direct the industries.

A visitor to an insane asylum saw three wardens take three hundred of the inmates out for exercise. The visitor expressed surprise at the perfect control which the three had over the three hundred. He asked for an explanation and was told that the three wardens were organized and that the three hundred insane were unorganized. That is, the three had their minds made up as to just what they wanted to do and did it. The three hundred did not have their minds made up. They did not care what they did nor what was done with them.

Society develops with the advance of science and the invention of machines. Industrial development produces ever higher forms of organization. We shall first discuss the growth and nature of the present or capitalist organization of industry.

At first, when machines are small and few, an industry is controlled by small capitalists. Individuals own the machines, the raw materials and perhaps the land on which, and the shop in which, the work is carried on. In this first stage the capitalist often works along with his employees. He at least is useful in that he directs industry. He buys the raw material. He superintends the shop. He sells the finished product. But even at this stage the portion he takes as profits is much greater than his part in production. His income is not at all determined by the work he performs. Let us see what does fix the amount he takes from the workers as profits and the amount he gives them as wages.

Wages and Profits.

When the capitalist employs the worker he of course pays as little in wages as possible. If the worker is skilled he will usually get more wages than if unskilled, because it required time and labor to develop his skill. If workers are scarce their price in the market will go up for a time. If, however, there are many unemployed, wages will decline. Wages are the price paid in the market for the labor power of the worker. The amount of wages does not depend at all upon the amount of the workers' product. On the average, wages amount to just enough to keep the worker in good shape for his work. If there were no great unemployed army, if machines did not constantly take the place of more and more workers, then the average male worker would have to receive enough to support a wife, and children to take the place of the parents. But the unemployed army and the new machines are constantly forcing wages in many industries down to a point below what is absolutely necessary to support a wife alone, not to mention children. Also, until about twenty years ago there was another factor in American life that tended to keep wages up. There was plenty of free land in the West. The strongest, boldest workers, especially those who had a little money in the bank, could always go West and take up free land or get a good job. In the West there was much work to be done and workers were scarce. As some left the East the wages of others went up or were prevented from going down. So there developed among the working people in America what has been known as "the American standard of living." But during the last twenty years American workers have been constantly getting less and less for their work.

How Wages Have Gone Down.

In dollars and cents the average wages have probably not gone down at all during the past fifteen years. In many cases they have actually risen. But measured by the food, clothing and shelter the worker can buy with his wages, which is the only true way to measure an income, wages have gone down at least fifty percent in this time. Prices have gone up not because the trusts are able to charge any price they please, but for a wholly different reason. Gold is our standard measure of value and gold is becoming ever cheaper and cheaper. It is now produced by machines and the cyanide process. As much gold can be turned out by two days' labor now as by three days' labor fifteen years ago. Therefore, when goods of any kind are sold in the market, it takes three dollars in gold today to buy as much as two dollars would buy formerly.

But wages, the price of labor power in the market, have not generally gone up. Mr. James J. Hill, one of the greatest railroad magnates in America, has declared that the time has come for the American people to live cheaper, like European peasants. That statement is absolutely true. The wages of the American worker have gone down one-third in fifteen years because he can no longer get away from his master. Machines are taking his place and he can no longer go West, take up government land and be free. Had the value of gold remained as it was, wages would have gone down just the same. Higher prices is simply a form which lower wages takes.

Nothing but Socialism can prevent the condition of the American workers from becoming just as bad as that of the working people of Europe, or even worse.

The Portion of Labor.

Wages are the price of the food, clothing and shelter needed by the worker who has the job. Profits are all that portion of the laborer's product which is left to the capitalist after the wages have been taken out. Let us suppose that a capitalist sells a year's product of his shop for $100,000. Suppose that raw materials and shop expenses amount to $25,000. The product of the workers in the shop is therefore $75,000. If there are fifty workers in the shop who receive, on the average, $500 a year, that would amount to $25,000 in wages. There is still left the sum of $50,000. That is profits and is pocketed by the capitalist, who may not have worked a single day in the shop or office. Now let us say that next year five machines are put in and that they replace forty workers. These five machines require only five workers. That means that fifteen workers will be left in the shop. Their wages, at $500 each, will be $7,500. So next year the capitalist will pocket $17,500 more in profits, or $67,500. By and by the starving workers who have lost their jobs will come back and offer to work for less. Wages are cut to $400 a year. That means $1,500 more in profits. At the present time this is just what is taking place everywhere in America. The percentage and amount of profits is getting to be greater and greater and greater, and, on the average, wages are getting to be less and less and less.

Profits do not go up because the capitalists do more. The manager's brains are under the workman's cap. In fact, as industry develops, the capitalist does less and less useful work. Profits go up because the capitalists own and control the industries.

Wages do not go down because the workers produce less. They are producing ever more and more. Wages go down and ever down, because the capitalist can buy the workers at ever cheaper and cheaper prices in the market. Wages are going down because machines are taking the place of workers; because women and children are leaving the home and working in the factories and offices; because the workers can no longer work for themselves but are chained in their master's service. Finally, wages go down because it takes less food, clothing and shelter to keep a worker alive today than his father required, demanded and received fifty years ago.

The Nature of a Capitalist.

The capitalists and their agents are constantly telling the workers that they got their start by saving their money and wisely investing it. A long time ago this may have been true in some cases. These few cases of capitalists who began honestly were constantly pointed out until the workers were led to believe that they could save some of their wages and start in business. Of course today the trusts are so powerful that very few workers are foolish enough to try to become capitalists. But many of them still believe the foolish tales the thieving capitalists tell about themselves. A capitalist does nothing except for profits. For more profits there is nothing he will not do.

The True History of Some of These Capitalists.

In Gustavus Myers' *History of the Great American Fortunes*, we find a true account of the lives of the most noted of the American capitalists. Mr. Myers has most carefully examined the records of courts and legislatures, family histories and newspaper files dealing with the subject.

For instance, the Astor family, which owns more than $400,000,000 worth of real estate in New York City, got its start through the fur trade with the Indians. The Astor agents committed a crime every time they gave the Indians liquor. But they regularly made the Indians drunk and often stole their furs. The founder of the family, John Jacob Astor, built up this great system of criminal trade and made millions. He then stole great quantities of real estate from the city of New York. In the War of 1812 his agent proved a traitor to his country, imparting valuable government secrets to the British in return for protection to the Astor properties in Canada. Since then the Astors have always carefully observed that passage of Scripture which reads: "Consider the lilies of the field, how they grow; they toil not, neither do they spin." Their fortune in valuable New York real estate grows while they sleep. But instead of being fed by the Heavenly Father they are being fed by the sweating working class of New York City.

The most powerful capitalist in America today is J. Pierpont Morgan. He is said to control ten billions of dollars. He himself possesses an estate worth $250,000,000.

How did he get it? Mr. Myers has told us.

In 1861 the government of the United States was everywhere hurriedly purchasing arms to put in the hands of its soldiers. Also it sold much worn-out material to make place for new. Among the junk offered for sale was a supply of 5,000 rifles in an arsenal in New York City. They were more dangerous to the men back of them than to those in front of them, as they would burst on the first fire. But this fact did not worry J. Pierpont Morgan. Instead of going to the front as a soldier he stayed at home and made money. Through an agent he purchased these rifles from the United States government at $3.50 apiece. He then resold them to the United States government at $25.00 apiece. The government paid him $17.50 for each rifle but refused, upon learning of Mr. Morgan's swindling game, to pay more. In 1864 the whole Nation was worn out by the awful Civil War. Most of the able bodied men, except a crowd of thieving, grafting capitalists who stayed at home and got rich, were in the army. Yet at that time, in the very crisis of the war, the unspeakable Morgan won his suit against the government and collected the extra blood money.

When, a few years ago, the "muckrakers" were exposing the crimes of the great capitalists, those who tried to defend them pointed to Russell Sage as a man of spotless honor, an ideal for American youth. Mr. Myers shows that Russell Sage, as a young man, started out in life by stealing a railroad. He then took the money made out of it and bribed the governor and legislature of Wisconsin into giving him valuable lands. So it is with all of them, the Vanderbilts, the Goulds and the Rockefellers. They get their great wealth not only by taking their profits from the workers directly. They degrade city, state and national governments by bribing the officials and using them in their business. They steal from one another. They rob the ignorant and the weak. But of course the greatest and most lasting injury done the workers consists in paying them wages as low as possible and taking as much profit as possible in the shops and mines and on the railroads where the workers toil.

No one ever produced $100,000,000 nor $1,000,000. If a man has any such amount of wealth he got it by grabbing and keeping profits out of the product of the workers. He may have gotten it directly from the workers, or indirectly by robbing other capitalists or gambling in the stock market.

The Social and Moral Difference Between Capitalist and Worker.

No worker should wish to become a capitalist. The small capitalist cannot thrive as a capitalist without lying and cheating; without paying low wages and sweating his workers through long hours, without lying awake nights planning how to help himself by injuring others.

The worker cannot rise as a worker without joining in unity with other workers and helping all. This mutual dependence of worker upon worker, taught them by their everyday experiences in the shop, is the best and finest thing in modern life. It leads to brotherhood. It develops the mind of the worker. It raises him out of a state of individual selfishness and meanness and points to the goal of civilization—Socialism.

The Corporation

The individual capitalist soon found that he was powerless to control the growing government of the shop, the mine and the store. The size and great number of the machines invented and the growing market due to railroads and other means of transportation led to this. These forces became too great for him to control through his own personal wealth. So there came the next higher form in the organization of industry—the corporation. A business corporation is an association of capitalists which, because of the rights granted to it by the government through its charter, can do business very much as does an individual. There were very great corporations which engaged in commerce long before modern machines were invented. The first English settlements in North America were made by such corporations as the Virginia Company and the Plymouth Company. So the corporation is a very old form of organization. But at first it was confined almost wholly to trade upon the high seas. Before the invention of machines there were but few corporations in the productive industries. In England, as we have already pointed out, machines began to be used in the making of cloth in 1764. They were not set up in America until about 1800. After that time corporations developed very rapidly. Soon, with the coming of machines, corporations were engaged in the production of iron, of lumber and of many other commodities. With the invention of the steamboat in 1807 and the railway in 1829, the size of the market which could be reached by a corporation grew to include the whole Nation. So the corporations developed rapidly in both numbers and in size. As long ago as when Andrew Jackson became President, in 1829, they became so powerful as to dictate the policies of the government at Washington. Andrew Jackson saw the danger. He saw how the old political government of the people was used by the new industrial government, the corporations. Although he smashed the most powerful of these, the great United States Bank, he could not stay the progress of industry. The corporations were bound to grow because the Nation's industries needed a government of their own. The working people were not prepared at that time to take over and own the machines of production. So they were owned and controlled by the rich. Of course many individual capitalists still owned factories, but no individual ever owned any railway line of any consequence. By 1861, when the Civil War broke out, the capitalist class, composed of individuals and corporations, was quite as strong as the great farming class. When the Civil War ended, in 1865, it had grown so rich through cheating the government, through high tariffs, high prices and low wages, that it was by far the most powerful class in the country.

The Coming Of The Trusts

When the modern Socialist Movement was first started, the Socialists aimed to do two things. First, they wished to abolish competition and establish co-operation. Second, they wished to have the working class so organized that they could control the machines of production and take the whole product. The first of these purposes was considered to be as important as the second. Competition was known to be a very great evil. It immensely increased the whole amount of work to be done. For instance, instead of having one fine large department store in a city of 25,000 people, the Socialists saw a hundred small stores. The Socialists saw the competing business men cheat one another and the public. They saw ten doing work which one could do. Surely this, said the Socialists, is a most foolish and wasteful way of doing business. Socialism would make an end of it. Socialism would bring about co-operation instead of competition. It would end competition not only in the store, but also in the shop.

Competition.

At this the small business men laughed and jeered. "Competition," said they, "is the life of trade. Everybody knows that. The Socialists are mostly lunatics and at best a lot of dreamers. Without competition there would be no business done and consequently nothing produced. Everyone would go naked and starve." So said the small shop keepers and factory owners forty years ago.

Then the natural growth of industry brought the trust. The trust is neither "bad" nor "good." It is simply natural, like a tree or a river. It comes when conditions force it to come. Those who organize a trust must do so in order to protect and advance their interests.

As the machine process develops, competition becomes instead of "the life of trade," much more the death of trade. Each competitor tries to outdo the others. He goes beyond his means. The markets are glutted with goods which the workers have produced but are too poor to buy from the capitalists. One competitor after another goes bankrupt. The shops become idle and the stores find no purchasers. This is called a "crisis" or a "panic." Meanwhile the workers are idle and the small business men are mired. Whole armies of people starve. It sometimes takes years to outgrow a panic.

With the growth of competitive industry, panics become worse and worse. The worst one we had in this country was that of 1893-8. The growth of railroads, the telegraphs and mail service had increased the range of the market to include the whole Nation. A small factory was brought into competition with all other factories turning out the same kind of goods. Among the railroads the words "competition" and "ruin" meant the same thing. Two or more competing lines would force one another to the verge of bankruptcy. Running expenses were cut. The railroad workers were shamelessly underpaid and overworked. The lives of the trainmen and of passengers were sacrificed as in war. When the owners of the railroads tried to abolish this foolish and dangerous competition, the ignorant people demanded laws forcing it to be continued.

There was only one thing to do. Trusts must be formed to control the markets. The first great group of trusts were organized in 1899.

What Is a Trust?

Trusts are formed in the following way. A number of the largest producers in any industry, both individuals and corporations, bring their holdings together. Suppose that one hundred separate pieces of property are to be taken in. A board of trustees is chosen. The owners agree upon a price, in each case, with this board of trustees. Then they place their properties in "trust" and receive stocks, bonds or money from the central organization. The trust is simply a later and better organization than the corporation. It is just as foolish to try to smash trusts as it would be to smash corporations and partnerships. The bigger the machines and the larger the market, the greater must be the organization of industry. The partnership may be compared to the formation of a family. Two people unite for their mutual welfare. A corporation is like a village or small town. Then comes a combine of corporations and individuals which resembles a county. Finally a trust is organized. A trust controls some branch or great department of industry. It may be compared to a state like New York, Missouri or California. Instead of controlling a definite section of the Nation's territory, it controls a branch of the Nation's industry.

How the Trust Becomes a Monopoly.

A trust in any industry starts with the largest and best factories and controls the widest markets. Perhaps it possesses also large supplies of raw materials, a part of which its small competitors must purchase. At first it is not likely to be a monopoly. It may not even control a majority of the trade. Suppose that it controls 30% and its smaller rivals, together, 70%. But the trust soon begins to swallow its competitors. It may undersell them in their markets. It hires their most able workingmen and selling agents. It secures valuable railroad rebates, an advantage in which the small producer cannot share. It spies upon the small producer until it knows just what he is doing and plans to do. Very soon most of the small producers are willing to give up the fight and sell out to the trust. If not, they are forced into bankruptcy. Thus the trust becomes a monopoly. Then comes its period of prosperity. As a monopoly a trust may often raise its prices considerably without endangering its hold on the market, for small competitors do not dare to start up again. They know that the trust will quickly lower prices in their district and again bring them to ruin.

The Trust and the Workers.

The trusts not only crush their business competitors. They are able to smash the old-fashioned unions which grew up in the days of small machines and small shops. These unions were composed of skilled workers. The progress of machine industry, making their skill unnecessary, destroyed their effectiveness, even as it did that of the small corporation. Only there is this difference. In place of the small corporation has come the trust. In place of the old-fashioned union the trust has, so far, permitted few new unions to grow. The most striking example of this is in the iron and steel industry. This gigantic trust possesses great mines, ships, railroads, steel plants and in some cases the towns in which the plants are located. It has

$1,400,000,000 of capital. It employs, when working to its full capacity, 200,000 workers. In the old days of small production the workers were protected by the Amalgamated Association of Iron and Steel Workers. This union secured the eight-hour day for many of its members. Today many of the slaves of the Steel Trust toil twelve hours a day, seven days a week. On the Great Lakes the Steel Trust has killed the Seamen's Union and made serfs of the sailors. In the Lake Superior mines the workers are not permitted to organize. They are not even permitted to hold public meetings for the discussion of their condition.

The Trusts Are Governments of Industry.

We have seen that the trusts grow naturally — that it cannot be otherwise. They can never be destroyed. There would in fact be only one possible way of making an end to them. That would be to smash the large machines of production and the great railway systems. The trouble is not that we have trusts. The workers' condition comes from the fact that the trusts are owned and governed by a few people. Very often they are dominated by one man. Thus Morgan governs the Steel Trust. Morgan can make a law increasing the hours or decreasing the wages. He can prevent the workers from protecting themselves in the factories and thus kill and injure thousands of them. In fact 560 steel workers were killed in the mills of Pittsburgh in a single year.

Industrial Tyranny.

The workers thus live under an awful tyranny. They are ruled without their consent. The government which oppresses them is the government of the shops, the mines and the railroads. This government declares when they shall work and when they shall be idle. All of the profits taken by the capitalist class are in reality taxes paid by the workers. These taxes are not voted by the workers. They are seized by the employers. The idea that we have freedom in America is ridiculous. What the capitalists call "freedom," is nothing but freedom to enslave the working class. This they can now do without let or hindrance.

The Industrial Empire Of America

We have compared the trust to an industrial state. Many states make up the Nation. In the same way many trusts compose our present great nation of industry. The trusts are rapidly organizing into one great system. So the Nation is coming to be governed as an empire. J. Pierpont Morgan is now the chief ruler of this empire. He is the emperor of the trusts. Under him there are kings and dukes who rule separate trusts and corporations. This great government of industry is said, upon very good authority, to have brought on the Panic of 1907 in order to seize several great corporations which were fighting it. During this panic it grabbed hundreds of small businesses.

No capitalist, even though he might possess ten million or twenty million of money, can today start any new business of his own unless he goes to Wall Street, appears at court, and gets the consent of the Emperor of America. Whatever small separate industries exist, still remain alive because the industrial empire does not wish to crush them out too fast. To do this would be to raise a cry of revolt among the middle class. Until now the workers have been so enslaved, so helpless, so deadened, that the Wall Street magnates have not even thought of their opposition seriously. But it would not do to go too far and too fast. So some small business men are still permitted to enjoy a hand-to-mouth existence.

The Industrial Empire and the Government at Washington.

Morgan and his associates on Wall Street use the government at Washington as a tool to serve their ends. They rightly despise the President, the members of the Supreme Court and Congress, for these politicians are far beneath them in power and importance. What laws Wall Street wants are passed. In case of a strike, the governor of a state is used to control the militia and crush the strike. The federal and state judges issue injunctions, that is, they make such new laws as the trusts want. The powers of the separate states are usually quite strong enough to deal with the divided and blinded working class. But if these do not suffice, then the powers of the National Government are used. Grover Cleveland, a Democratic President, broke the great A.R.U. strike in 1894. Theodore Roosevelt, a Republican President, broke the Goldfield Miners' strike in 1907. The Republican state of Pennsylvania has established a standing army of its own in order to have it ready to shoot working people. The Democratic legislature of Florida, in the spring of 1911, refused to pass a law forbidding the employment of children under eight years of age. All the Democratic and Republican officials, from dog-catcher to President, are but the hired agents of the empire of industry.

The Real Government of the United States of America is governed from Wall Street, New York. This is the real seat of public power. Under its tyrannical laws all of us are forced to live. When labor raises its head it is quickly clubbed into submission. The industrial oligarchs are now attempting to destroy freedom of speech and of the press. Professors in the universities and colleges and teachers in the public schools do not attempt to tell the truth about government. Such as do quickly lose their positions. Clergymen and priests do not dare preach the truth about the working class in their sermons, for the industrial empire is gaining control of the churches. All of the newspapers in the larger cities, except the Socialist papers, are owned out and out by the capitalists. They are used to keep the workers in ignorance and to entertain them with pictures, cheap sporting news and sensational reports of scandals.

Thus the trusts control the army, the navy, the police, the political government, the schools, the press, the church, and even the theaters. The industrial empire is a power with its forces encamped in every city and state of the land, armed not only with the weapons which slay the body, but also with those mightier weapons which destroy the free mind of the working class. Is all hope lost? Let us see.

The Organization Of Labor

Capitalists cannot live without wage-workers. Where one class exists there the other will be found. Furthermore, there is sure to be trouble between the two. The master is always scheming to get more profits out of the worker. The worker fights for more wages from his boss. The less one gets the more there is for the other. Hence we have, between the capitalist and his worker, what is known as the Class Struggle.

At first this struggle does not seem to be important. The small capitalist and his workers associate together and may for a time be good personal friends. This small capitalist is not very rich nor is the worker very poor. The personal relationship between the two prevents violent outbreaks. At this stage of production, especially in America, the more greedy and calculating workers were constantly "rising" and becoming small capitalists.

But with every step in the growth of industry, peace between the capitalist and worker becomes less likely. Soon the capitalist lives an altogether different life from the worker. He associates only with his own kind. He builds himself a palace and travels about the world. Meanwhile the worker continues to work and sweat in the shop. Neither he nor any of the members of his family meet the capitalist or his family. The capitalist's children go to college. The worker's children go to work.

The Growth of the Class Struggle.

And thus the two classes come to be wholly separated as regards every aspect of life. The capitalist who never works comes to despise work and the workers. The worker naturally hates the capitalist who is taking such huge profits and paying such low wages. But at first the worker's opinions are not clear in his own mind. In fact, few workers even now understand the real problem which confronts them.

The Problem of Labor.

However, it was very early discovered that the only way for the workers to make head against the capitalists was to organize. The purpose of labor unions has been to control, or partly control, the conditions of labor and the division of labor's product. That is, the workers seek, through their unions, to help govern the industries, instead of letting the capitalist do just as he pleases. Every demand made by organized labor upon the capitalists is in the nature of a proposed law for the shop. When the capitalist surrenders and gives in to the demands of the workers the law is passed.

The Two Kinds of Labor Unions.

From the beginning of the labor union movement in America, about 1825, there have always been two views as regards the methods and purposes of unions. Some unionists always wished to organize only the skilled workers in small groups and thus advance the price of their labor. Such unions are craft unions or trade unions. These do not care much for the interests of the working class as a whole. They merely wish to help themselves to better conditions. If only the capitalists give in to their demands, they may continue to oppress members of other crafts or unorganized workers as much as they please. Of course so long as the members of a craft may better their condition in this way there is no argument against craft unionism. Craft unions will exist as long as they are successful.

Early Class Unionism.

But another kind of unionism in some form or other has always, from the beginning, been advocated. This is class unionism. A class union is one which attempts to unite all the workers against all the capitalists. It recognizes the fact that all the workers are suffering from the same cause. It sees the capitalists, whenever driven to it by their interests, unite solidly against the workers. And usually the advocates of class unionism have been wise enough to foresee that if the workers wish permanent relief from wage-slavery they must secure complete control of the industries. But when this doctrine was first advocated in America, eighty years ago, the time was not ripe for it. The machines were too small, the markets were too limited, and therefore capitalism was not highly enough organized. It was at that time a beautiful and inspiring vision of what the future was to bring, rather than a practical policy for the working class.

The Growth of the Craft Unions.

The great error of the craft unionists has been in thinking that they can permanently better the condition of all the members of their craft. The skilled worker can generally sell himself in the open market for only a little more than the unskilled worker, at most from ten to twenty percent more. Let us take, for example, a machinist. A man of average intelligence can learn the machinist trade in three years. If the machinists receive very much more than the average of the unskilled workers, large numbers of the unskilled will set themselves to becoming machinists. By and by the number of machinists will outrun the number of jobs to be had. Then the wages of the machinists will fall until it is but little more than that of unskilled labor.

To meet this difficulty the craft unionists do not attempt to keep up wages chiefly by fighting the employers. They seek to make of their union a job trust. This is done, first, by restricting the number of apprentices. Some unions permit only the sons and brothers of the members to learn their trade. But this method cannot be entirely successful. The employers will always find ways of securing more skilled workers. Some come from other countries. But most of the newcomers in the trade are those who have been helpers. Thus blacksmiths' helpers soon become blacksmiths and machinists' helpers become machinists. Time and again have these trades gone on strike only to find that their helpers have taken their places and done their work. There remains but one thing for the union to do. It may keep out new members by high initiation fees and closed books. This is very commonly done and the union scale of wages for a time maintained. But it cannot be permanent. Sooner or later, in every trade, comes the machine. The machine is the great leveler. It has broken the ranks of union after union by making an end of the trade. In the few remaining crafts where high wages are paid and the eight-hour day is maintained, as in the building trades, there are so many workers that unemployment brings down the average yearly wage to far below the union scale. Also, while the cost of living goes up fifty percent, the craft union may raise wages twenty percent. There appears to have been a rise when in fact there has been a fall in wages. In the face of all these facts craft unions cannot maintain the standard of living of their members.

But the greatest weakness of craft unions flows from the very nature of their organization and purpose. The American Federation of Labor, which includes nearly all of the craft unions of the Nation, never at any time claimed to have had more than seven percent of the American working class within its ranks. It does not exist for the purpose of organizing the working class. It is a loose association of craft unions, each of which merely desires to keep up the standard of wages and hours in its own trade. The American Federation of Labor has no message for the working class. It does not seek to make an end of unemployment, of child labor, and of all the other frightful conditions of labor. To accomplish this it would have to make an end of the wages system. It would have to fight the capitalists as a matter of principle. But instead of fighting the capitalists, craft unionism whenever possible makes peace with them and supports the wages system. Out of this attitude grows one of the greatest errors of craft unionism, the signing of agreements with the employers. These agreements tie the hands of the workers and prevent them from striking for better conditions. But they do not prevent the capitalist from shutting up his shop and turning the workers into the street whenever he pleases. There should be no agreements between capitalists and wage workers which bind the workers to their work. Like the blind, the craft unions hobble along a step at a time, seeing not where they go. Every new invention of machinery makes the journeyman of today the apprentice of tomorrow. While industrial progress is destroying union after union, those that remain hug the delusion that they are going to last forever. It was of these unions that Karl Marx said forty-six years ago that they generally failed "from limiting themselves to a guerilla war against the effects of the existing system instead of trying to change it, instead of using their organized forces for the abolition of the wages system."

The Growth of the Class Unions.

In all of the particulars above enumerated, class unionism is the opposite of craft unionism. The early form of the class union movement in the United States was the Knights of Labor. It was organized in 1869. It rose to its period of greatest strength from 1880 to 1890 and practically went out of existence in 1895. Its position was fundamentally correct. It sought to bring together all workers in one big union. It kept steadily before it a great general principle—the universal eight-hour day. But the Knights of Labor, as regards two matters, was in error. First, while it provided for one big union for all the workers, it permitted no industrial departments nor craft locals within the union. It gathered into one local the butcher, the baker and the candlestick maker. There are often separate problems of industrial departments, and sometimes of craft locals, which the whole union cannot solve so well as the members of the particular industry or craft affected. In failing to provide for industrial shop organizations, the Knights of Labor paved the way for its own destruction. Secondly, the Knights of Labor admitted to its ranks small capitalists, members of the professions and other non wage-workers. This was a very great error. A union should contain only members of the working class.

Instead of making peace with the capitalist whenever it can, class unionism fights the capitalist whenever it can. Instead of being satisfied with the present enslaved condition of the working class, class unionism has always for a goal a permanently better condition for all the workers. Today industrial unionism, which is the form class unionism has taken, must agitate ceaselessly for the emancipation of the working class.

Industrial Unionism.

The motto of industrial unionism is "One union of all workers in an industry; all industries in one union." The question is not what tool do you use, but what kind of product do you help turn out? Industrial unionism has been developed to meet the conditions confronting the workers since the coming of the latest machines and the organization of the trusts.

The revolutionary industrial union is ever active; always fighting. The prosperity of a modern labor organization is measured by its activity. Activity for improved conditions or against the lowering of existing standards of living means that the membership is in arms against the exploiters.

Action against exploitation requires agitation, publicity, strikes, boycotts, political force—all the elements and expressions of discontent. Discontent is life. It impels to action. Contentment means stagnation and death.

The Western Federation of Miners.

As an example of what industrial unionism can do we shall briefly trace the history of the most successful of all American labor unions, the Western Federation of Miners. It was organized in 1892 for the purpose of bringing together all the workers in the industry of metal mining in the United States. It united the man who used the pick and shovel and the man who used the machine. It included the engineers, the mill and smelter men and all other workers in and about the metal mines.

This union of course developed strength absolutely impossible among craft unions. When a strike is declared all the workers strike at once. Agreements with the bosses are never signed. The Western Federation of Miners never furnishes the ridiculous spectacle of one part of its members being on strike against the employer and another part at work breaking the strike. This form of organization helped to develop the fighting spirit for which the Western Federation of Miners has been noted. Where the interest of each is the concern of all, a spirit of genuine solidarity prevails. No strike can be long and bitter enough to dishearten the miners.

By fighting a series of the greatest battles in the history of American labor, the Western Federation of Miners has won the eight-hour day, not for a few craft unionists, but for all the workers in and about the mines, skilled and unskilled alike. It has obtained almost everywhere the minimum wage of $3.00 a day, and in many mining towns the minimum wage is $3.50. Where wages go up it is found that it is much easier to raise those of the skilled laborer higher than where the unskilled are unorganized and unprotected. For instance, where the unskilled worker received $3.50, the machine runner $4.00 and the engineer $5.00, the pick and shovel men are not all struggling to become machine runners and engineers.

The General Strike.

There are three phases of a general strike. They are:

A general strike in an industry,

A general strike in a community, or

A general national strike.

The right conditions for any of the three on a large scale have never existed. So no one can logically take the position that a general strike would not be effective and not be good tactics for the working class. We know that the capitalist uses the general strike to good advantage. Here is the position that we find the working class and the capitalists in: The capitalists have wealth. They have money. They invest the money in machinery and in the resources of the earth. They operate a mine, a factory, or a railroad. They keep that factory running just as long as there are profits coming in. When anything happens to disturb the profits, what do the capitalists do? They go on strike. They withdraw their financial support from that particular mill. They close it down because there are no profits to be made there. They care not what becomes of the working class. But the working class, on the other hand, has always been taught to take care of the capitalist's interest in the property. It cares too little for its own interests. A general strike would ignore the capitalist's interests and concern itself with the workers' interests only.

Power in the Industries.

The industrial organization is capable not only of the general strike. It prevents the capitalists from disfranchising the workers in the shops. It gives the vote to women. It re-enfranchises the black men and places the ballot in the hands of every boy and girl employed in a shop, making them eligible to take part in the general strike. It makes them eligible to legislate for themselves where they are most interested in changing conditions, namely, in the place where they work.

Industrial Unionism Grows.

At the present time practically the whole American working class accepts the principles of industrial unionism. All agree that the workers should have one big union. All are coming to agree that this union must more and more control industry, until finally it rules and administers the industries of the Nation. When the working class is well enough organized industrially and possesses the necessary political power, it will take its whole product. The capitalists must then go to work. Socialism will thus be a reality. Everywhere the idea arouses intense enthusiasm. The growth and progress of industrial organization itself must soon follow. Once united, industrially and politically, and resolved to make an end of wage slavery, nothing can prevent the final victory of the workers.

IV— Industrial Freedom

Socialism is industrial democracy.

Industrial democracy is Socialism.

Under Socialism the government of the Nation will be an industrial government, a shop government. The political government of today, composed of president, congress and the courts, with the governments of the various states, is purely a class government. It is the government of the property holding classes. Its purpose is to protect private property and keep the workers, who have no property, in subjection. Its most important laws are laws of oppression. Its most important buildings are court houses and prisons. Its most important servants are policemen, detectives and soldiers.

Socialism, or shop government by the workers, will need no armies, navies, police, detectives and prisons. Judges today are almost wholly concerned with two kinds of work. One is to try cases at law which grow out of private property relations. When two property holders quarrel about a piece of property they go to court in order to have the fight settled as cheaply as possible. Another function of the courts is to sit in judgment upon, and determine the punishment of, such of the poor as may have been "guilty" of disrespect for private property. Of course everybody now knows that rich offenders purchase this "justice," while poor offenders get it presented to them. Do the starving poor take food? They are sent to jail. Do they strike for more wages? They are clubbed, shot or imprisoned. Such is the nature and purpose of the political government today.

Under Socialism there will be no lawless rich to keep their place by crushing the poor. There will be no enslaved poor to be kept down. There will be no great private fortunes to fight about in the courts. Hence government will concern itself only with the management of industry, with the promotion of public education and with other public activities which are of benefit to the workers.

The Growth Of Socialism

Unity of the Labor Union and the Socialist Party.

The Socialist Party and the labor union will come closer and closer together. The labor union will come to stand for Socialism. The Socialist Party will thus become a mere phase of the labor movement. The union and the party together make war upon the enemy, the capitalist class. This fight is, first of all, a shop fight. It takes place at the point of production where the workers are at present enslaved. Until this is understood there can be no real understanding of Socialism. To understand the world and the world's struggle at the present time we must look at it through shop windows. That is why college professors, preachers, authors and business men must take the working class point of view before they can understand Socialism. They must understand the struggle in the shop. Then only can they understand the needs of the workers and the power of the workers. Otherwise these upper class people will be weak-kneed reformers and not Socialists. Many clergymen, college professors and lawyers, and workers who have learned their Socialism from these, imagine that Socialism is "government ownership." "Under Socialism," they say, "the government will own the railroads, the mines and the factories."

Government Ownership Not Socialism.

Government ownership can never lead to Socialism. It is not a step toward Socialism. It has nothing Socialistic about it, because all political government is administration from the top. At the present time the employees of the United States Post Office are treated worse than many employees of private capitalists. The railway mail clerks are less protected and work for less wages than most of the other trainmen. Wherever the capitalists are being driven by the Socialist Movement they are crying out for "government ownership" to save them. The railroad thieves in the United States will soon want nothing so much as to turn over their watered stocks to the National Government. They would then draw their profits as interest on government bonds. No profits in the world could be safer. The government would then have to rob the railroad workers and turn over the stolen money to the idle government railroad bondholders.

The present governments of the United States and of the separate states were developed long before Socialism was thought of. Even if the workers put Socialists of proved wisdom and honesty in office, the present government could not possibly become a Socialist government. It was not made for that purpose. The workers might as well take a cannon left over from the Revolutionary War, run it on the street car track and pretend that it is an up-to-date electric car, as to try to make over the present government of the United States into a Socialist government. A wise tailor does not put stitches in rotten cloth.

The political government of capitalism has served its purpose. Its day is done. The Socialist Party can seize it, prevent its doing further harm to the workers and at the proper time throw it on the scrap heap where it will repose with the outworn tools for the protection of which it was organized.

The Industrial Empire.

We have already described the new government—the government of industry. Its development began with the organization of industrial corporations. At the present time it is rapidly becoming centralized. Its capital is at New York City. There its executive and legislative departments are located. It is a plutocracy, a form of government by the great rich. It is rapidly becoming an empire.

This industrial government makes the real laws of the land. It determines who shall and who shall not work and how long and for what wages. That is, it has the power to say who shall live and who shall not live. It legislates as regards the amount of protection the worker shall receive while at work. It holds in its hands the powers of both the industrial and political governments. It has decreed, in order that profits may be increased, that the workers shall suffer slavery, starvation, disease and death.

The Industrial Republic.

The workers' government of the future will realize Socialism. No government is created in a day. Any new system of society, with its peculiar government, must grow through many years to its final and perfected form. In this, Socialism cannot be different from other forms of government. Socialism cannot be realized until the workers, through their industrial government, own and manage the means of production. This government is now developing—in the workshops, of course. Wherever the organized workers gain partial control over the shop in which they work, we have the growth of industrial democracy. If the workers have been employed twelve hours a day and they force their employer to grant them the ten-hour day, they are passing an important law of the shop. That law springs from the power of the workers to govern the shop.

Suppose that the workers of the whole Nation demanded and enforced the eight-hour day. That would be a mightier law in the interest of the working class than all the laws ever passed by Congress and the state legislatures.

With the growth of the organized industrial and political power of the workers, the class struggle will become ever keener. The government of the capitalists will make war on the workers. The battle will rage throughout the land, in every city and town, in every shop and mine. It will continue until the workers are strong enough to gain complete control of the Nation's industries. The trust is organized industry. The labor union will become organized industrial society.

The Class Struggle In Politics

In their war upon the working class, one of the most effective weapons of the capitalists has been the physical force wielded by their political government. Everywhere the workers have been fooled into supporting this government. The Republican and Democratic parties and the various reform parties are maintained to keep the workers divided. Whichever of these capitalist parties is victorious, the workers are always defeated. Democratic, Republican and reform politicians alike use the powers of government in the interests of the master class, wherever the workers seek to control the shop. Whenever the workers strike they are brutally clubbed, stabbed and shot by police and soldiers. Whenever they declare a boycott they may be put in jail. Injunctions prevent them from picketing a struck shop and talking to the strikebreakers. The courts seize the funds of the union and turn them over to the capitalists.

Fortunately the male workers have the right to vote. At first they foolishly try to defend themselves by defeating this or that obnoxious politician of the old parties. They vote for such politicians as call themselves "the friends of labor." But they soon find out again that "the friends of labor" out of office, become the enemies of labor when in office. So finally, in every country under the sun, the workers are forced to organize a party of their own.

The Socialist Party.

In America this party of the workers is the Socialist Party. It has now been developing for nearly twenty years. For many workers it seems to grow too slowly. This is because of the great work and mission of the Socialist Party. A labor reform party might elect officers very quickly and in a few years control the country. In Australia this has actually taken place. But the workers of Australia have found that their Labor Party is no better than any other capitalist party. This is so because it is not a Socialist party. The Socialist Party stands not merely for the *political* supremacy of labor. It stands for the *industrial* supremacy of labor. Its purpose is not to secure old age pensions and free meals for school children. Its mission is to help overthrow capitalism and establish Socialism.

What Will the Socialist Party Do?

The great purpose of the Socialist Party is to seize the powers of government and thus prevent them from being used by the capitalists against the workers. With Socialists in political offices the workers can strike and not be shot. They can picket shops and not be arrested and imprisoned. Freedom of speech and of the press, now often abolished by the tyrannical capitalists, will be secured to the working class. Then they can continue the shop organization and the education of the workers. To win the demands made on the industrial field it is absolutely necessary to control the government, as experience shows strikes to have been lost through the interference of courts and militia. The same functions of government, controlled by a class-conscious working class, will be used to inspire confidence and compel the wheels of industry to move in spite of the devices and stumbling blocks of the capitalists.

The Socialist Party is not a political party in the same sense as other parties. The success of Socialism would abolish practically every office existing under the present form of government. Councils, legislatures and congresses would not be composed principally of lawyers, as they are now, whose highest ambition seems to be to enact laws with loop-holes in them for the rich. But the legislatures of the workers would be composed of men and women representing the different branches of industry and their work would be to improve the conditions of labor, to minimize the expenditure of labor-power, and to increase production.

The Message Of The Socialist Party

The most priceless intellectual possession of the world's workers has been the gift of the Socialist Movement. This includes a complete system of thought with regard to human society and social progress. It was worked out by the first great scientific Socialists, Karl Marx and Frederick Engels. Their main ideas are included in this system. We shall briefly discuss each of these.

Surplus Value.

Long before the coming of the modern Socialist Movement it was understood by the economists that all wealth is produced by labor. How then, it was questioned, can profits be accounted for? If labor produces all wealth why do not the laborers receive their full product? The answer to this question was not known until it came from Karl Marx. Wages, said Marx, are not the full product of labor. Nor are wages any definite part of the product. Wages are simply the selling price of the worker in the market. This selling price, on the average, is just enough to keep the worker in good condition to do his work and produce someone to take his place. For instance, if the worker toils ten hours and produces $10.00 worth of wealth, he does not receive $10.00, nor $5.00. If $2.00 will support him he receives $2.00, and no more. These $2.00 are his wages and the remaining $8.00 are the profits of the capitalist. If the hours of the worker be increased, and better machines introduced, the workers' product is increased, let us say, to $15.00. Do the workers' wages go up? No. They are now but $1.50. The profits, or surplus-value, are now $13.50.

The theory of surplus value is the beginning of all Socialist knowledge. It shows the capitalist in his true light, that of an idler and parasite. It proves to the workers that capitalists should no longer be permitted to take any of their product. Without this knowledge the worker will never fight along correct lines. With this knowledge he will never stop fighting until Socialism, which will give to the working class the whole of its product, shall be fully realized.

Economic Determinism.

Until Marx it was generally thought that history was made by great men. Great men won battles, made treaties of peace, created constitutions and laws, ruled nations, and saved humanity from destruction. Marx and Engels showed, through their study of history, that this was a childish view of life and of government. The great facts of history—its wars, its governments, its art, science and literature— these were created by a deeper social force. This force, said Marx, was the economic or material force. People lived as they did and acted as they did, because they made their living in a certain way. If they used small, rude tools, and the soil they worked was poor, their ideas would be much different from what they would be if they used larger and more productive tools upon richer soil. The nature of man's social life depends chiefly upon the physical conditions under which he is living. This same principle is true in matters of morality. An individual, or nation, or a class, will finally come to think that right which is to his material advantage. Nations make war in order to add to their possessions.

Individuals engage in such work, or business as will yield them the largest pay or profits. A class will fight to the death with another class over profits or wages.

In war, killing people and burning cities is thought to be a patriotic work. If successful it is considered to be right and fine. In industry the capitalists will enslave small children, and the profits wrung from their pitiful toil goes to build churches and universities and support Christian missions. The murderous capitalist who robs cradles to get his gold comes to be praised as most "benevolent," "virtuous," "religious," etc.

When the worker, either through experience or a study of Socialism, comes to know this truth, he acts accordingly. He retains absolutely no respect for the property "rights" of the profit-takers. He will use any weapon which will win his fight. He knows that the present laws of property are made by and for the capitalists. Therefore he does not hesitate to break them. He knows that whatever action advances the interests of the working class is right, because it will save the workers from destruction and death. A knowledge of economic determinism places the worker squarely on his intellectual feet and makes him bold and independent of mind.

The Class Struggle.

An understanding of the class struggle, which we have repeatedly discussed before, comes only from a knowledge of the economic interpretation of history. If the conditions of a people are determined by the nature of the tools they use, of the work they do, and by their relation to these tools (that is, whether they own them or not), then we may easily obtain an insight into the working class struggle. All the great revolutions of history, said Marx, have been class struggles. So, too, must be the movement of the workers. No class has been really free until it has ruled society. Therefore the working class, to be free, must rule society. But the workers, when they free themselves, will make slaves of no one. Machines will be so developed that everyone can labor and live in freedom. Long ago slavery was necessary to the end that the master might develop civilization. Under Socialism a higher and better civilization will be open to all.

The Growth of the Socialist Party.

The necessity and value of a knowledge of Socialism to the working class need not be emphasized. Into every country has gone the Socialist Party with its message of enlightenment and hope. This part of its work has just begun. In America, on April 1, 1911, eighty thousand people had accepted the principles of Socialism and joined the Party. In 1910, its candidates received 600,000 votes. But millions remain to be educated to a knowledge of Socialism before freedom can be obtained. In this work both the Socialist Party and the labor union will bear a prominent part. During the political campaigns the educational work of the Party is especially effective. It can then get the ear of the working class and emphasize the great truths it bears. Political victories are themselves of great value in drawing the attention of the working class to Socialism and spreading a desire to understand it.

The Socialist Party and the Government of Cities.

The Socialist Party has a further function. Modern industrial cities are a product of Capitalism. They are growing and will continue to grow constantly larger. The governments of cities are much more than the agents of the capitalist class. They develop social service departments, such as the fire department, the waterworks, public schools and parks. Through a department of public health, they can, by means of scientific hygiene, protect and promote the health of the community.

These governments of cities are at present run by politicians, in the interests of the capitalists, for graft. They must be captured and used in the interest of the workers. But at present, city government in the interest of the workers is made almost impossible through the capitalist control of the states. With the growth of the Socialist political power they can more and more be liberated to serve the working class.

The mission of the Socialist Party is therefore three-fold:

First, it must lay hold of all the powers of political government and prevent them from being used against the industrial organization of the workers.

Second, it must be the bearer of sound knowledge, using its great and growing organization to teach Socialism.

Third, it must use the governments of the cities to advance the social interests of the working class.

The Socialist, through his knowledge of the law governing social progress, gains an insight into the future which is impossible to those ignorant of Socialism. Through his study of history he comes to understand the part played by revolutions. Whenever a social class has become powerful enough to rule society it has seized the reins of government. Thus the capitalist class in western Europe and America has made an end of the power of kings. They have accomplished this through a number of revolutions. The most important of these were the English Revolution in 1642, the French Revolution in 1789, and the American Revolution in 1776. The Civil War in the United States was a very great revolution. It made an end of the power of the Southern slaveholding class and established capitalism in the South.

When the working class is strong enough both in its union and at the ballot box, it will make an end of capitalism. The period in which it will be engaged in the work of seizing all the powers of industrial and political government will be the period of the social revolution. Of course we cannot tell when this will come. Neither can we tell whether the period of revolution will be long or short. Both will depend upon several facts. The most important question is how long will it take to educate and organize the working class? This will be determined much by what the capitalists will do. The revolution might be hastened by a financial panic. It might be retarded by a foreign war or by capitalist reforms. But it is bound to come. That the well-informed Socialists can clearly see.

The Immediate Demands of the Workers.

There is only one sense in which it can be said that Socialism will be realized "a step at a time." The steps taken must move the workers on toward control of the industries. The workers can today demand and enforce the eight-hour day, protection of life and limb, and abolition of sweating and driving. The labor union should emphasize the present fight in the industries. The Socialist Party should emphasize the workers' goal — revolution, Socialism and complete freedom.

Political States Merged by Industry.

The separate states of the United States have long since ceased to be needed. At one time the people of different states were widely separated because it took so long to travel from one to another. Now they are connected by railroads, telegraph, the post office and by the trusts and labor unions. An old-fashioned farmer would inherit his father's farm and leave it to his son. His family were permanent citizens of the state in which he lived. But the members of the working class move from state to state in search of employment, caring little in which one they happen to be. Let us say that a worker is employed by the Pennsylvania Railroad Company. His employer is the state of which he is a member, and which governs him. He may live in New York, New Jersey, Pennsylvania, or any of six other political states. As a trainman he goes through them but does not recognize their boundaries.

Similarly, a worker for the Grand Trunk Railway in Canada may live in Michigan, Ontario or New York. But the place of his residence is not important at all when compared with the province of the Grand Trunk system to which he is subject. The great Smelter Trust extends its operations from the United States into Canada and Mexico. Canada and Mexico are parts of the American industrial empire. The Western Federation of Miners has more locals in British Columbia than in any American state. Members of the W. F. of M. go back and forth over the Canadian border, working often for the same trust on both sides of the line and supporting always the same union. So with Industrial Socialism. It will recognize no political boundary lines. To the working class there is no foreigner but the capitalist.

No Socialism but Industrial Socialism.

Socialist government will concern itself entirely with the shop. Socialism can demand nothing of the individual outside the shop. It will not say to the worker how he shall use his product. Socialism has absolutely nothing to do with either religion or the family. It has no concern with the numberless social reforms which the capitalists are now preaching in order to save their miserable profit system. Old age pensions are not Socialism. The workers had much better fight for higher wages and shorter hours. Old age pensions under the present government are either charity doled out to paupers, or bribes given to voters by politicians. Self-respecting workers despise such means of support. Free meals or cent meals for poverty-stricken school children are not Socialism. Industrial freedom will enable parents to give their children solid food at home. Free food to the workers cuts wages and kills the fighting spirit.

When a worker understands Industrial Socialism, he does not ask who will do the hard work, will Socialism divide up, will Socialism destroy incentive, and similar foolish questions. Yet some serious questions remain to be answered. When Socialism is explained as a political scheme, to be brought about by the passing of laws in the legislatures and Congress, these questions are naturally many and hard. But Industrial Socialism is Socialism with its working clothes on. It is easily understood by the workers. As we look from shop windows upon the world about us, the questions which come into our minds about Industrial Socialism are few and simple.

The Time and Duration of Work Under Socialism.

Everybody now realizes that it is ridiculous for sane people to work all day and every day. "The less work the better," is the motto which the workers must set themselves. Let the immense profits which now go to the capitalists be taken by the workers. Let all the lawyers, most of the physicians, the drummers, and the host of small storekeepers and the unemployed workers but go to work and produce wealth. Let all the wealth now wasted in wars, in strikes, in competitive business—let all this waste stop. Let the newest and best machines and scientific methods be everywhere used. Let the intelligence of the workers be liberated for the many inventions and the development of better processes, which would rapidly follow under Socialism. If all this were to be done, it is readily seen that a small portion of the day, or a few days per month, or a few months steady work per year, will yield wealth in abundance. It would be foolish for us to say how much a worker should work, because we do not know how much wealth he will desire for himself and his family. It is not for us to determine that. But it is most reasonable to suppose that under Socialism an individual working eight hours a day for four months in the year will produce food, clothing and shelter in abundance for a family of five people.

Votes for Women.

Socialist government will be a democratic government of industry by all the workers. Of course both men and women will work. Free people do not wish to be supported, nor support idlers and parasites. Therefore, when those who work rule, women will take part in government.

Those Who Will Not Work.

Those who will not work will probably not be permitted to starve. They will undoubtedly be tenderly cared for in insane hospitals and nursed back to health. At present, even, all healthful people wish to work, yet none desire life-long slavery to the profit of others.

The Coming Freedom

In the shop there must be government. In the school there must be government. In the conduct of the great public services there must be government. We have shown that Socialism will make government throughout democratic. The basis of this freedom will be the freedom of the individual to develop his powers. People will be educated in freedom. They will work in freedom. They will live in freedom. Most of the diseases which now afflict humanity will be unknown because their causes will have been removed. Where there is plenty for all, none will be driven to swindle, to steal or to take profits. Higher education will be within the reach of every one. Science and the arts will flourish.

Socialism will establish democracy in the shop. Democracy in the shop will free the working class. The working class, through securing freedom for itself, will liberate the race. Socialism will free not only the slave but the slave-driver and the slave-owner. Socialism today makes war upon the enemies of the working class. When it is victorious, the enemies of the working class will embrace it. Peace and brotherhood will come with freedom.

The General Strike

Speech by William D. Haywood

New York, March 16, 1911

Comrades and Fellow Workers: I am here tonight with a heavy heart. I can see in that Raymond Street jail our comrade and fellow-worker Buccafori in a cell, a miserable cell, perhaps 4 ½ feet wide, 7 feet long, sleeping on an iron shelf, wrapped up in a dirty blanket, vermin-infested perhaps; surrounded by human wolves, those who are willing to tear him limb from limb, those who will not feel that their duty to the political state is entirely fulfilled until Buccafori's heart ceases to beat. I had felt that this would be a great meeting. I feel now that I would hate to be in Buccafori's place. It is better, when charged with crime by a capitalist or by the capitalist class, to hold a prominent office in a great labor organization. You will then draw around you support—support sufficient to protect and to save your life.

Had I been an ordinary member of the rank and file of a labor organization no more prominent than a shoe worker of Brooklyn I would not be here tonight. I am certain that I would be sleeping in a bed of quicklime within the walls of the Idaho State penitentiary. But it happened that I was a prominent official of a labor organization that was known world-wide; and for one to raise his voice in defense of the officials of that organization meant to give the speaker prominence. To speak in favor of Buccafori is to come into an out-of-the-way part of town and to speak to a small audience. There are those who prefer prominence to saving a fellow-worker's life. I came here tonight to do my little part, feeling that Buccafori is as much to the labor movement, is as much to the working class, is as beneficial to society as I myself, as any member here, or any of those who ever lifted their voice for me.

I am sorry that I haven't supernatural strength to reach into that prison and release Buccafori. I am sorry that I can't bring together the forces that saved my life. I can only speak here as an individual.

I came tonight to speak to you on the general strike. And this night, of all the nights in the year, is a fitting time. Forty years ago today there began the greatest general strike known in modern history, the French Commune; a strike that required the political powers of two nations to subdue, namely, that of France and the iron hand of a Bismarck government of Germany. That the workers would have won that strike had it not been for the co-partnership of the two nations, there is to my mind no question. They would have overcome the divisions of opinion among themselves. They would have re-established the great national workshops that existed in Paris and throughout France in 1848. The world would have been on the highway toward an industrial democracy, had it not been for the murderous compact between Bismarck and the government of Versailles.

We are met tonight to consider the general strike as a weapon of the working class. I must admit to you that I am not well posted on the theories advanced by Jaures, Vandervelde, Kautsky, and others who write and speak about the general strike. But I am not here to theorize, not here to talk in the abstract, but to get down to the concrete subject whether or not the general strike is an effective weapon for the working class. There are vote-getters and politicians who waste their time coming into a community where 90 percent of the men have no vote, where the women are disfranchised 100 percent and where the boys and girls under age, of course, are not enfranchised. Still they will speak to these people about the power of the ballot, and they never mention a thing about the power of the general strike. They seem to lack the foresight, the penetration to interpret political power. They seem to lack the understanding that the broadest interpretation of political power comes through the industrial organization; that the industrial organization is capable not only of the general strike, but prevents the capitalists from disfranchising the worker; it gives the vote to women, it re-enfranchises the black man, and places the ballot in the hands of every boy and girl employed in a shop, makes them eligible to take part in the general strike, makes them eligible to legislate for themselves where they are most interested in changing conditions, namely, in the place where they work.

I am sorry sometimes that I am not a better theorist, but as all theory comes from practice you will have observed, before I proceed very long, that I know something about the general strikes in operation.

Going back not so far as the Commune of Paris, which occurred in 1871, we find the great strike in Spain in 1874, when the workers of that country won in spite of combined opposition against them and took control of the civil affairs. We find the great strike in Bilboa, in Brussels. And coming down through the halls of time, the greatest strike is the general strike of Russia, when the workers of that country compelled the government to establish a constitution, to give them a form of government — which, by the way, has since been taken from them, and it would cause one to look on the political force, of Russia at least, as a bauble not worth fighting for. They gave up the general strike for a political constitution. The general strike could and did win for them many concessions they could gain in no other way.

While across the water I visited Sweden, the scene of a great general strike, and I discovered that there they won many concessions, political as well as economic; and I happened to be in France, the home of all revolutions, during the strike on the railroads, on the state as well as the privately owned roads. There had been standing in the parliament of France many laws looking toward the improvement of the men employed on the railroads. They became dissatisfied and disgruntled with the continued dilatory practices of the politicians and they declared a general strike. The demands of the workers were for an increase of wages from three to five francs a day, for a reduction of hours and for the retroaction of the pension law. They were on strike three days. It was a general strike as far as the railroads were concerned. It tied up transportation and communication from Paris to all the seaport towns. The strike had not been on three days when the government granted every demand of the workers. Previous to this, however, Briand had issued his infamous order making the railroaders soldiers— reservists. The men went back as conscripts; and many scabs, as we call them over here (I don't know what the French call them; in England they call them "blacklegs"), were put on the roads to take the places of 3,500 discharged men.

The strike apparently was broken, officially declared off by the workers. It's true their demands had all been granted, but remember there were 3,500 of their fellow-workers discharged. The strikers immediately started a campaign to have the victimized workers reinstated. And their campaign was a part of the general strike. It was what they called the *"greve perlee,"* or the "drop strike"—if you can conceive of a strike while everybody is at work; everybody belonging to the union receiving full time, and many of them getting overtime, and the strike in full force and very effective. This is the way it worked—and I tell it to you in hopes that you will spread the good news to your fellow-workers and apply it yourselves whenever occasion demands—namely, that of making the capitalist suffer. Now there is only one way to do that; that is, to strike him in the place where he carries his heart and soul, his center of feeling—the pocketbook. And that is what those strikers did. They began at once to make the railroads lose money, to make the government to lose money, to make transportation a farce so far as France was concerned. Before I left that country, on my first visit—and it was during the time that the strike was on—there were 50,000 tons of freight piled up at Havre, and a proportionately large amount at every other seaport town. This freight the railroaders would not move. They did not move it at first, and when they did it was in this way; they would load a trainload of freight for Paris and by some mistake would be billed through to Lyons, and when the freight was found at Lyons, instead of being sent to the consignee at Paris it was carried straight through the town on to Bayonne or Marseilles or some other place—to any place but where it properly belonged. Perishable freight was taken out by the trainload and sidetracked. The condition became such that the merchants themselves were compelled to send their agents down into the depots to look up their consignments of freight—and with very little assurance of finding it at all. That this was the systematic work of the railroaders there is no question, because a package addressed to Merle, one of the editors of "La Guerre Sociale," now occupying a cell in the Prison of the Saint, was marked with an inscription on the corner "Sabotagers please note address." This package went through posthaste. It worked so well that some of the merchants began using the name of "La Guerre Sociale" to have their packages immediately delivered. It was necessary for the managers of the paper to threaten to sue them unless they refrained from using the name of the paper for railroad purposes.

Nearly all the workers have been reinstated at the present time on the railroads of France.

That is certainly one splendid example of what the general strike can accomplish for the working class.

Another is the strike of the railroaders in Italy. The railroaders there are organized in one great industrial union, one card taking into membership the stenographers, train dispatchers, freight handlers, train crews and section crews. Everyone who works on the railroad is a member of the organization; not like it is in this country, split up into as many divisions as they can possibly get them into. There they are all one. There was a great general strike. It resulted in the country taking over the railroads. But the government made the mistake of placing politicians in control, giving politicians the management of the railroads. This operated but little better than under private capitalism. The service was inefficient. They could make no money. The rolling stock was rapidly going to wreck. Then the railroad organizations issued this ultimatum to the government, and its now stands: "Turn the railroads over to us. We will operate them and give you the most efficient service to be found on railroads in any country." Would that be a success for the general strike? I rather think so.

And in Wales it was my good fortune to be there, not to theorize but to take part in the general strike among the coal miners. Previous to my coming, or in previous strikes, the Welsh miners had been in the habit of quitting work, carrying out their tools, permitting the mine managers to run the pumps, allowing the engine winders to remain at work, carrying food down to the horses, keeping the mines in good shape, while the miners themselves were marching from place to place singing their old-time songs, gathering on the meeting grounds of the ancient Druids and listening to the speeches of the labor leaders; starving for weeks contentedly, and on all occasions acting most peaceably; going back to work when they were compelled to by starvation. But this last strike was an entirely different one. It was like the shoemakers' strike in Brooklyn. Some new methods had been injected into the strike. I had spoken there on a number of occasions previous to the strike being inaugurated, and I told them of the methods that we adopted in the West, where every man employed in and around the mine belongs to the same organization; where, when we went on strike, the mine closed down. They thought that that was a very excellent system. So the strike was declared. They at once notified the engine winders, who had a separate contract with the mine owners, that they would not be allowed to work. The engine winders passed a resolution saying that they would not work. The haulers took the same position. No one was allowed to approach the mines to run the machinery. Well, the mine manager, like the mine managers everywhere, taking unto himself the idea that the mines belonged to him, said, "Certainly the men won't interfere with us. We will go up and run the machinery." And they took along the office force. But the miners had a different notion and they said, "You can work in the office, but you can't run this machinery. That isn't your work. If you run that you will be scabbing; and we don't permit you to scab—not in this section of the country, now." They were compelled to go back to the office. There were 325 horses underground, which the manager, Llewellyn, complained about being in a starving condition. The officials of the union said, "We will hoist the horses out of the mine."

"Oh, no," he said, "we don't want to bring them up. We will all be friends in a few days."

"You will either bring up the horses now or you will let them stay there."

He said, "No, we won't bring them up now."

The pumps were closed down on the Cambria mine. 12,000 miners were there to see that they didn't open. Llewellyn started a hue and cry that the horses would be drowned, and the king sent the police, sent the soldiers, and sent a message to Llewellyn asking "if the horses were still safe." He didn't say anything about his subjects, the men. Guarded by soldiers, a few scabs, assisted by the office force, were able to run the pumps. Llewellyn himself and his bookkeeping force went down and fed the horses.

Had there been an industrial organization comprising the railroaders and every other branch of industry, the mines of Wales would be closed down today.

We found the same condition throughout the West. We never had any trouble about closing the mines down; and could keep them closed down for an indefinite period. It was always the craft unions that caused us to lose our fights when we did lose. I recall the first general strike in the Coeur d'Alenes, when all the mines in that district were closed down to prevent a reduction of wages. The mine owners brought in thugs the first thing. They attempted to man the mines with men carrying six-shooters and rifles. There was a pitched battle between miners and thugs. A few were killed on each side. And then the mine owners asked for the soldiers, and the soldiers came. Who brought the soldiers? Railroads manned by union men; engines fired with coal mined by union men. That is the division of labor that might have lost us the strike in the Coeur d'Alenes. It didn't lose it, however. We were successful in that issue. But in Leadville we lost the strike there because they were able to bring in scab labor from other communities where they had the force of the government behind them, and the force of the troops. In 1899 we were compelled to fight the battle over in a great general strike in the Coeur d'Alenes again. Then came the general strike in Cripple Creek, the strike that has become a household word in labor circles throughout the world. In Cripple Creek 5,000 men were on strike in sympathy with 45 men belonging to the Millmen's Union in Colorado City; 45 men who had been discharged simply because they were trying to improve their standard of living. By using the state troops and the influence of the Federal government they were able to man the mills in Colorado City with scab millmen; and after months of hardship, after 1,600 of our men had been arrested and placed in the Victor Armory in one single room that they called the "bullpen," after 400 of them had been loaded aboard special trains guarded by soldiers, shipped away from their homes, dumped out on the prairies down in New Mexico and Kansas; after the women who had taken up the work of distributing strike relief had been placed under arrest—we find then that they were able to man the mines with scabs, the mills running with scabs, the railroads conveying the ore from Cripple Creek to Colorado City run by union men—the connecting link of a proposition that was scabby at both ends! We were not thoroughly organized. There has been no time when there has been a general strike in this country.

There are three phases of a general strike. They are:

A general strike in an industry;
A general strike in a community; or
A general national strike.

The conditions for any of the three have never existed. So how any one can take the position that a general strike would not be effective and not be a good thing for the working class is more than I can understand. We know that the capitalist uses the general strike to good advantage. Here is the position that we find the working class and the capitalists in. The capitalists have wealth; they have money. They invest the money in machinery, in the resources of the earth. They operate a factory, a mine, a railroad, a mill. They will keep that factory running just as long as there are profits coming in. When anything happens to disturb the profits, what do the capitalists do? They go on strike, don't they? They withdraw their finances from that particular mill. They close it down because there are no profits to be made there. They don't care what becomes of the working class. But the working class, on the other hand, has always been taught to take care of the capitalist's interest in the property. You don't look after your own interest, your labor power, realizing that without a certain amount of provision you can't reproduce it. You are always looking after the interest of the capitalist, while a general strike would displace his interest and would put you in possession of it.

That is what I want to urge upon the working class; to become so organized on the economic field that they can take and hold the industries in which they are employed. Can you conceive of such a thing? Is it possible? What are the forces that prevent you from doing so? You have all the industries in your own hands at the present time. There is this justification for political action, and that is, to control the forces of the capitalists that they use against us; to be in a position to control the power of government so as to make the work of the army ineffective, so as to abolish totally the secret service and the force of detectives. That is the reason that you want the power of government. That is the reason that you should fully understand the power of the ballot. Now, there isn't anyone, Socialist, S. L. P., Industrial Worker or any other workingman or woman, no matter what society you belong to, but what believes in the ballot. There are those—and I am one of them— who refuse to have the ballot interpreted for them. I know, or think I know, the power of it, and I know that the industrial organization, as I stated in the beginning, is its broadest interpretation. I know, too, that when the workers are brought together in a great organization they are not going to cease to vote. That is when the workers will *begin* to vote, to vote for directors to operate the industries in which they are all employed.

So the general strike is a fighting weapon as well as a constructive force. It can be used, and should be used, equally as forcefully by the Socialist as by the Industrial Worker.

The Socialists believe in the general strike. They also believe in the organization of industrial forces after the general strike is successful. So, on this great force of the working class I believe we can agree that we should unite into one great organization— big enough to take in the children that are now working; big enough to take in the black man; the white man; big enough to take in all nationalities — an organization that will be strong enough to obliterate state boundaries, to obliterate national boundaries, and one that will become the great industrial force of the working class of the world. (Applause.)

I have been lecturing in and around New York now for three weeks; my general topic has been Industrialism, which is the only force under which the general strike can possibly be operated. If there are any here interested in industrial unionism, and they want any knowledge that I have, I will be more than pleased to answer questions, because it is only by industrial unionism that the general strike becomes possible. The A. F. of L. couldn't have a general strike if they wanted to. They are not organized for a general strike. They have 27,000 different agreements that expire 27,000 different minutes of the year. They will either have to break all of those sacred contracts or there is no such thing as a general strike in that so-called "labor organization." I said, "so-called;" I say so advisedly. It is not a labor organization; it is simply a combination of job trusts. We are going to have a labor organization in this country. And I assure you, if you could attend the meetings we have had in Philadelphia, in Bridgeport last night, in Haverhill and in Harrison, and throughout the country, you would agree that industrialism is coming. There isn't anything can stop it. (Applause.)

Questions by the Audience.

Q. — Don't you think there is a lot of waste involved in the general strike in that the sufferers would be the workers in larger portion than the capitalists? The capitalist class always has money and can buy food, while the workers will just have to starve and wait. I was a strong believer in the general strike myself until I read some articles in *The Call* a while ago on this particular phase.

A. — The working class haven't got anything. They can't lose anything. While the capitalist class have got all the money and all the credit, still if the working class laid off the capitalists couldn't get food at any price. This is the power of the working class: If the workers are organized (remember now, I say "if they are organized" — by that I don't mean 100 percent, but a good strong minority), all they have to do is to put their hands in their pockets and they have got the capitalist class whipped. The working class can stand it a week without anything to eat — I have gone pretty nearly that long myself, and I wasn't on strike. In the meantime I hadn't lost any meals; I just postponed them. (Laughter.) I didn't do it voluntarily, I tell you that. But all the workers have to do is to organize so that they can put their hands in their pockets: when they have got *their* hands there, the capitalists can't get theirs in. If the workers can organize so that they can stand idle they will then be strong enough so that they can take the factories. Now, I hope to see the day when the man who goes *out* of the factory will be the one who will be called a scab; when the good union man will stay in the factory, whether the capitalists like it or not; when we lock the bosses out and run the factories to suit ourselves. That is our program. We will do it.

Q. — Doesn't the trend of your talk lead to direct action, or what we call revolution? For instance, we try to throw the bosses out; don't you think the bosses will strike back?

Another thing: Of course, the working class can starve eight days, but they can't starve nine. You don't have to teach the workingman how to starve, because there were teachers before you. There is no way out but fight, as I understand it. Do you think you will get your industrialism through peace or through revolution?

A. — Well, comrade, you have no peace now. The capitalist system, as peaceable as it is, is killing off hundreds of thousands of workers every year. That isn't peace. One hundred thousand workers were injured in this state last year. I do not care whether it's peaceable or not; I want to see it come.

As for starving the workers eight days, I made no such program. I said that they could, but I don't want to see them do it. The fact that I was compelled to postpone a few meals was because I wasn't in the vicinity of any grub. I suggest that you break down that idea that you must protect the boss's property. That is all we are fighting for—what the boss calls his "private property," what he calls his private interest in the things that the people must have, as a whole, to live. Those are the things we are after.

Q.—Do the Industrial Unionists believe in political action? Have they got any special platforms that they support?

A.—The Industrial Workers of the World is not a political organization.

Q.—Just like the A. F. of L.?

A.—No.

Q.—They don't believe in any political action, either, so far as that is concerned.

A.—Yes, the A. F. of L. does believe in political action. It is a political organization. The Industrial Workers of the World is an economic organization without affiliation with any political party or any non-political sect. I as an Industrialist say that industrial unionism is the broadest possible political interpretation of the working-class political power, because by organizing the workers industrially you at once enfranchise the women in the shops, you at once give the black men who are disfranchised politically a voice in the operation of the industries; and the same would extend to every worker. That to my mind is the kind of political action that the working class wants. You must not be content to come to the ballot box on the first Tuesday after the first Monday in November, the ballot box erected by the capitalist class, guarded by capitalist henchmen, and deposit your ballot to be counted by black-handed thugs, and say, "That is political action." You must protect your ballot with an organization that will enforce the mandates of your class. I want political action that counts. I want a working class that can hold an election every day if they want to.

Q. — By what means could an Industrial Unionist propagate Industrial Unionism in his organization of the A. F. of L.? He would be fired out and lose his job.

A. — Well, the time is coming when he will have to quit the A. F. of L. anyway. And remember that there are 35,000,000 workers in the United States who can't get in the A.F. of L. And when you quit you are quitting a caste, you are getting back into your class. The Socialists have been going along maintaining the Civic Federation long enough. The time has almost arrived when you will have to quit and become free men and women. I believe that the A. F. of L. won't take in the working class. They don't want the working class. It isn't a working-class organization. It's a craft organization. They realize that by improving the labor power of a few individuals and keeping them on the inside of a corral, keeping others out with initiation fees, and closing the books, and so on, that the favored few are made valuable to the capitalists. They form a little job trust. It's a system of slavery from which free people ought to break away. And they will, soon.

Q. — About the political action we had in Milwaukee: there we didn't have Industrial Unionism, we won by the ballot; and while we haven't compelled the government to pass any bills yet, we are at it now.

A. — Yes, they are at it. But you really don't think that Congressman Berger is going to compel the government to pass any bills in Congress? This Insurgent bunch that is growing up in the country is going to give you more than the reform Socialists ever asked for yet. The opportunists will be like the Labor Party in England. I was in the office of the Labor leader and Mr. Whiteside said to me: "Really, I don't know what we are going to do with this fellow, Lloyd-George. He has taken every bit of ground from under our feet. He has given the working class more than the Labor Party had dared to ask for." And so it will be with the Insurgents, the "Progressives" or whatever they propose to call themselves. They will give you eight-hour laws, compensation laws, liability laws, old-age pensions. They will give you eight hours; that is what we are striking for, too—eight hours. But they won't get off the workers backs. The Insurgents simply say "It's cruel, the way the capitalists are exploiting the workers. Why, look! Whenever they go to shear them they take off a part of the hide. We will take all the wool, but we will leave the hide." (Laughter.)

Q. (By a woman comrade)--Isn't a strike, theoretically, a situation where the workingmen lay down their tools and the capitalist class sits and waits, and they both say, "Well, what are you going to do about it?" And if they go beyond that, and go outside the law, is it any longer a strike? Isn't it a revolution?

A.—A strike is an incipient revolution. Many large revolutions have grown out of a small strike.

Q.—Well, I heartily believe in the general strike if it is a first step toward the revolution, and I believe in what you intimate— that the workers are damn fools if they don't take what they want, when they can't get it any other way. (Applause.)

A.—That is a better speech than I can make. If I didn't think that the general strike was leading on to the great revolution which will emancipate the working class I wouldn't be here. I am with you because I believe that in this little meeting there is a nucleus here that will carry on the work and propagate the seed that will grow into the great revolution that will overthrow the capitalist class.

Q.—How do you account for the course of the Western Federation of Miners in applying for a charter in the A. F. of L.?

A.—I wish I knew just what happened to the Western Federation of Miners when they asked for a charter from the A. F. of L. However, it's only in the shape of an application. The A.F. of L. did nothing for us while we were in jail, but the local unions that comprise the A. F. of L.'s membership did a great deal in the way of moral support, and they furnished a great deal of money. That trial cost $324,000--my trial. I don't look worth that much, but I am in my own estimation. Of the total amount the outside organizations contributed $75,000, the Western Federation of Miners put up nearly $250,000. There was a tremendous agitation throughout the country and the officials of the organization felt that the trade unions had come to them in a crisis and that they ought to join hands with the A. F. of L. movement. I feel that they assisted in that crisis, but it wasn't through the trade union machine—it was through the working class. Gompers never said a word until a Socialist in the central labor body here made him open his mouth. The officials of the trade unions never came to our relief. It was the Socialists, the S.L.P.'s, the I.W.W.'s, some trade-unionist members of local unions, local officials. It wasn't the machine. So, while I feel and I know I owe my life to the workers of the nation, it is to the working class of the nation that I am under obligation, not to any subdivision of that class. That is why I am here now. That is why I am talking working-class solidarity, because I want to see the working class do for themselves what they did for me.

Q.—What do you think about the Socialist movement in Germany?

A.—I think I know something about Germany, and if you want my opinion I will say that the Socialist movement in Germany seems to me to be a top-heavy one; that is, that the force comes from the top down—that is not a purely democratic movement, coming from the working class up.

Q.-Is it the capitalist class, or is it a labor movement, or both combined, or some conditions in between them that has anything to do with the insurrection in Mexico?

A.—I think the capitalist class are responsible for the insurrection in Mexico. Incidentally, the revolutionists, Magon,

Villareal, Sarabia and Rivera, and their followers, have something to do with it, as also the local unions of the Industrial Workers of the World, there now being at this time three locals whose entire membership have gone across the line and joined the insurgents, and Berthold, one of the commandants, is an officer in the I.W.W. at Holtville, Cal. So that they have something to do with the insurrection. But the revolution in Mexico has been brought on by the capitalists, and it was no snap judgment on the part of Taft, the sending of the troops to the Mexican border. You recall two years ago Elihu Root went down to Mexico to visit Mr. Diaz, and following Root's visit, on the 16th of October a year ago, Mr. Taft went down and met with Diaz in Juarez and El Paso. Here is, to my mind, the nut of it, here is the milk in that coconut: the Japanese have been crowding into Mexico ever since the Japanese said they wouldn't come to the United States. They have been coming into Mexico in swarms, until now the administration looks on with a great deal of dread as to just what it means, if there is going to be a Japanese war, with the little brown fellows right down there in Mexico ready to come across the border.

Again, Mr. Taft would like to extend the territory of the United States by benevolent assimilation down to the Isthmus of Panama. He would like to take in all of Mexico and Central America. Why? Because the interests of this country—when I say "the interests" I mean the big ones, the Standard Oil and the Morgans, and even the fellows on the undercrust, like Bill Hearst—have got vast interests down in Mexico. Not that it cost them a great deal of money. Hearst has a million and a half acres down there that he estimates to be worth $12,000,000, and he paid perhaps half a million for it. But their interests are there. Mexico is a wonderful country. The remarkable thing is that the capitalists have let it go as long as they have. It is a wonder they hadn't jumped on Mexico as the dons of Spain did, because there is no country under the sun that is as rich as Mexico. Central America is a marshy country, but in Mexico you come to the highlands and the plateaus; and that country, situated as it is, a narrow land between the Gulf of Mexico and the Gulf of

California and the Pacific, gets the benefit of the atmospheric precipitation, the benefit of the waters from both sides, so that they have plenty of rain, and can raise crops of everything — from rubber, cocoa, cotton, the tropical fruits, to the very hardest of wheat. The primeval forests in Mexico are second to nothing except the jungles of Africa. There they have great forests of mahogany, of dragonsblood wood, ironwood, copal, juniper and cedar that have never been touched. Just at this stage the reading of Prescott's *Conquest of Mexico* would be very interesting, also Humboldt's and Buckle's. The latter book I found to be perhaps not as exhaustive as Prescott's, but splendidly written.

Those I read while I was on my vacation, when I didn't have anything else to do but read. (Laughter.)

The capitalists, who are responsible for all wars are responsible for the present trouble in Mexico. (Applause.)

On the Case of
Ettor and Giovannitti

Speech by William D Haywood, May 21, 1912

Comrades And Fellow Workers:

It was the rumble of just applause that gave me courage and strength when I was in the same position as the men in whose behalf we are appealing to you tonight. I feel that my life must have been preserved by you for such occasions as this; and I feel now that it is not me to whom you are giving this magnificent reception, but the principles for which I stand. (Applause). Your applause is but an echo of your hearts, but an echo of your own desires; and you realize that the men who are in jail at Lawrence, are in jail because they are fighting your battles. I felt that when I was in jail in Boise. And I know that without the united action of the workingmen and women of New York City, of the state of New York, of the United States of America and of the world, instead of appealing to you here tonight on behalf of Ettor and Giovannitti, my comrades and I would have been judicially murdered by the authorities of the State of Idaho. The mine owners of Colorado, like the woolen and cotton kings of Massachusetts and the New England states, had determined to bring about our death, even as these vultures of capitalism intend to make horrible examples of Ettor and Giovannitti.

The Victory At Lawrence

We have heard and are hearing much of the wonderful victory of the strike in Lawrence. Whatever was achieved there in the way of victory was not accomplished by Ettor and Giovannitti alone; not accomplished alone by the men and women and children who went to make up that one big union of the working class; but the success of the Lawrence strike was largely due to the support and the influence of the socialist movement of America. (Applause).

It was you who came to our relief. When we made an appeal for financial aid it was the socialists who sent nearly three-fourths of all the funds that were raised during that strike. It was the working class of New York City, of Philadelphia, of Manchester and Barre, many of whom were socialists, who took care of the children during the long period of that industrial war. Without the support of the socialists, the strike of Lawrence could never have been won. (Applause). Without the support of the socialist movement, no strike in America can be won. (Applause). And without the support, without the influence, without the power of this great movement, Ettor and Giovannitti would be helpless tonight. But they have a right to expect your support. They are of your class. They are a part of the working class movement of America. They have devoted their lives to improving the condition of the downtrodden and the submerged, the unskilled and the unorganized, the common and the despised laborer. Yes, they are entitled to your support; and I know by your response here and by the response that you will give in the future and by the work that you will do among your fellow workers in the workshop and in your socialist locals, that Ettor and Giovannitti are once again to see the sunlight and to carry the message of socialism to the working class.

What Ettor And Giovannitti Did

I remember the last occasion of my speaking in this hall. It was a discussion between Comrade Hillquit and myself. We were not agreed on that occasion as to all points. We are agreed tonight. At the time of that discussion Joseph Ettor occupied a seat in the audience. He had a telegram in his pocket. You will remember, it was the 11th of January. That telegram was urging him to come to Lawrence. It came from that small part of the working class that had already been organized by the Industrial Workers of the World. It stated that a strike was imminent. Ettor felt that he ought to leave that night. He had some work to do. After leaving the meeting he corrected a manuscript on a debate that he had had some time previous. He sat up all night. And the next day he left for Lawrence.

The strike was then unorganized—the workers were in a state of chaos. Ettor showed a wonderful ability, a remarkable personality, a magnetism that few men are endowed with. It was Joseph J. Ettor, supported by Arturo Giovannitti, who brought together that great mass of humanity in Lawrence, Massachusetts: 27 different nationalities, speaking 48 different dialects, organized into one big union; melted, welded, amalgamated so strongly together that the capitalist class with all their machinations were unable to make even a dent in it.

Cause Of The Lawrence Strike

The strike, as you know, was against a reduction of wages. The legislature of Massachusetts, a meddling lot of reformers, without taking into consideration at all what it meant, passed a law reducing the hours of labor of women and children from 56 to 54 hours a week—not taking into consideration the men. The mill owners, without drafting any laws, on their part immediately tried to displace the women in the mills—they were more than 50 percent— by employing men, it being their intention to work the men 12 hours day and 12 hours night shift. But the supply of men in the New England states has about been exhausted. There were not enough to take the places of the women. As many as there were, were employed. The mill owners, without drafting laws, reduced wages when the 54-hour law went into effect; they put their thieving fingers into the envelopes of 30,000 mill workers and from each and every envelope extracted an amount that averaged 30 cents for each individual.

All For Thirty Cents

Thirty cents is a small sum, not enough to turn a world upside down about. But for 30 cents they turned Lawrence upside down. They put a hole through Schedule K, that changed the complexion of presidential candidates. They made some presidential candidates look like 30 cents. Thirty cents amounted to a great deal to the textile workers. It was the difference between life and death. You will think that this statement is somewhat exaggerated. Knowing that these people must have been receiving some wages, certainly they could have lived on 30 cents less. But remember: 30 cents was the difference between life and death. You remember the children that were sent to you to take care of, the first 119. When they arrived in New York they were taken to the headquarters of the Socialist Party on 84th street and after a repast they were critically examined by a corps of physicians. It was found, as a result oft such examination, that every one of those 119 children was suffering from malnutrition, that is, starvation. And it was not the result of three or fours days' hunger, but it was a chronic condition. Those children had been starving from birth. They had been starved in their mothers' wombs. And their mothers had been starving before the children were conceived.

A Common Organ With Common Needs

When the workers discovered that they had been robbed of another 30 cents — and it was but continuation of robberies that reduced them to the terrible condition that they were in — something told them that action was necessary. They had no common tongue. They could not understand each other. They had been gathered together by the cupidity of the mill owners as an old sea captain selects his crew of many tongues, so that there could be no coming together of minds, so that there could be no conspiracy, no mutiny, no strike, no understanding. But the mill owners overlooked the fact that each one of their workers was equipped with an organ that spoke the same in all languages, and that recognized no religion, no color, no nationality. They were equipped with a stomach. And they knew that 30 cents less in their envelopes meant a corresponding shrinkage in their stomachs. They knew that 30 cents less in the envelopes meant that some of their children were that much nearer death.

And it was the Italians who shouted, *"Viva let sciopero!"* The Syrians responded, and all the other workers joined in. They went out of the Wood mill. They went to the Washington mill and they took all the workers with them. And from there they went to the Lower Pacific mills. They approached the bridge across the canal; the mill owners seemingly had provided themselves for such an occasion. They had a hydrant on the outside of the mill, guarding the approach of the bridge. On this hydrant was affixed hose; and streams of hot and cold water were turned upon the strikers. They were drenched to the skin. It made them mad. They were excited, incited. They went to a car loaded with palings and they took those sticks of lumber and they went into the mill and they broke the machinery; they smashed the windows; they tore the fabric out of the looms. They destroyed much machinery, a few hundred dollars' worth (laughter), as much perhaps as a gang of Harvard students would destroy in one night's debauch celebrating the winning of a football game.

The Coming Of The "Gray Wolves"

But it was enough. It was the excuse that the mill owners wanted. They called on the mayor for the police. And the mayor sent what police he had. And the mill owners called again. And the mayor sent the fire department to take the place of policemen. Again they called. The mayor sent all the detectives. And he called on the governor for police. And the metropolitan police that we call the "gray wolves" came. They came from Boston, from Haverhill, from Salem, from Lynn, from Lowell. The town was crowded with police. And the mill owners were hollering for more police. And the mayor went to the saloons and gathered up all the bums, the material out of which police are made even in times of peace (Applause), and he put a star upon the breast of each one of these noble sons of Massachusetts, a club in their hand and a six-shooter in their pocket, and he started them against the strikers.

Dogs And Children!

The strikers had gotten all over their excitement. They were no longer angry. They were marching the streets with bands of music: the Syrians with their drum corps with its thrilling Oriental tunes. The strikers kept step. No thought of trouble. But the mill owners, particularly Mr. Burrell of the Duck mill, kept calling on the mayor for the militia, calling on the governor for the militia. Mr. Burrell was the manager of the mill of which Mr. Turner is president. The mere name "Mr. Turner" will not signify anything to you. Mr. Turner is a man of many wives and some wards. He married the last ward after he got rid of his wives. She lived in Brooklyn. They took their honeymoon. It was to Chicago. They had a palace train. Two Pullman cars were reserved for the bride's dogs. When those two carloads of dogs arrived in Chicago with their mistress they were taken to a fashionable hotel, registered, assigned to private rooms and were fed on the choicest cuts of meat; porterhouse steak. Dogs eating porterhouse steak while the little children of Lawrence were starving to death!

This was the man that wanted the militia. He is the kind of man who owns the militia. He is the kind of man who uses the militia to protect them in their licentious luxury.

The militia came. And it came to Lawrence, as it goes everywhere, to protect the property of the capitalist class. It did not come to police the town of Lawrence. There was no need of police. The people were quiet. But it came to protect the brick and steel that go to make up the equipment of the mills. And they came, as militia always come, with murder in their hearts. (Applause). And they committed murder.

The Murderous Militia

They killed John Rami, a Syrian boy, 16 years old, too young to die; a bright beautiful boy. He was out on the picket line that morning with other members of the band to which he belonged. He had a cornet in his hand—the only weapon. A soldier told him to move on. He didn't understand the English language well, but saw by the movements of the soldier that he meant that he should go. He turned and was walking up the sidewalk when the soldier plunged a bayonet in his back. It pierced his lung. He fell to the sidewalk. They took him to the hospital, and a few minutes after his arrival John Rami expired, the first martyr of the Lawrence strike.

Annie LoPizzo

It was only a few days after that the police killed Anna LoPizzo. The picket line was out that morning, 23,000 strong, an endless chain of pickets. And the police began to crowd them; crowded them up Common Street, up Union Street, down

Broadway, until they were massed in so thick that they could not move back any further. Then the policemen began to club them. Some of the sympathizers threw coal from the windows. The strikers themselves threw snowballs and chunks of ice at the policemen. And one of the policemen was hit with a chunk of coal or a chunk of ice on the leg. It was the sergeant. He ordered the policemen to pull out the guns. And as they did, they fired. And officer Benoit is said to have fired the shot that killed Anna LoPizzo. Nineteen witnesses saw him fire the shot. Anna LoPizzo died, the second martyr to the Lawrence strike.

The second day after she was killed, Joseph J. Ettor and Arturo Giovannitti were arrested for being accessories to her murder. Ettor or Giovannitti would willingly have laid down their lives to have saved the life of Anna LoPizzo. (Applause.) It was they who shed tears when they learned that Anna LoPizzo had been killed. They were two miles away at the time, speaking at the German meeting. Today they are in jail. They were held without bail, although there was no witness to say that they had had anything to do with the killing of Anna LoPizzo. There was no witness to say that Joseph J. Ettor or Arturo Giovannitti had ever spoken an inflammatory word all during the Lawrence strike.

The Workers' Only "Violence"

To read the record of the Lawrence strike is to acknowledge that the Industrial Workers of the World is pure in heart, that its conscience is clear and that its hands are clean of any violent work. (Applause). In that strike the workers knew their power. They were organized to exert that power. And the power that they possessed, was their productive power. Though foreigners not having a franchise, most of them women, many of them children—still they had their economic power. They had their labor power. They had the only power that you have got. The only capital that you have got is the one which is done up in your own hide. And they had just as much of that, more valuable to the mill owners than yours would be, because they were skilled in that particular line of work. And they committed no violence except that of removing their hands: big hands, delicate hands, baby hands; some of them gnarled and torn and crippled. But they removed those hands from the machinery. And when they took those hands away from the wheels of machinery the machinery was dead. (Applause).

And that was the "violence" of the Lawrence strike. And there is nothing more violent, in the eyes of the capitalist class, than to deprive them of the labor power out of which they get all their capital. There is nothing that will make the capitalist class so mad, that will make them froth at the mouth so quickly, as to see a working man with his hands in his pockets, or a working woman with her arms folded, or the little children playing with their dolls or their tops or their marbles. If they belong to the working army they want all those hands busy. Not to see them busy means that the golden stream has ceased to run into their coffers. And this is what makes the capitalist class crazy. (Applause). This is what has driven them mad. They see that while we realize that we have a tremendous political power and we are every year preparing ourselves to use that political power, there are those of us who also understand the tremendous significance of the power of our labor (applause); of the industrial organization; there are those of us who know that the foreigners in Lawrence have no vote because they have not been here long enough; and we know that the women couldn't vote, because Massachusetts is not in China; and we know that the children could not vote, that though they were old enough to work, they were not old enough to say under what conditions they should work. So the only power that they had was to organize on the industrial field and withdraw from the mills their economic power that the mill owners had been so ruthlessly exploiting. And they went on strike.

A Wonderful Strike!

It was a wonderful strike, the most significant strike, the greatest strike that has ever been carried on in this country or any other country. Not because it was so large numerically, but because we were able to bring together so many different nationalities. And the most significant part of that strike was that it was a democracy. The strikers handled their own affairs. There was no president of the organization who looked in and said, "How-dydo." There were no members of an executive board. There was no one the boss could see except the strikers. The strikers had a committee of 56, representing 27 different languages. The boss would have to see all the committee to do any business with them. And immediately behind that committee was a substitute committee of another 56 prepared in the event of the original committee's being arrested. Every official in touch with affairs at Lawrence had a substitute selected to take his place in the event of being thrown in jail.

All the workers in connection with that strike were picked from material that in the mill was regarded as worth no more than $6 or $7 a week. The workers did their own bookkeeping. They handled their own stores, six in number. They ran eleven soup kitchens. There were 120 investigating cases for relief. They had their own finance committee, their own relief committee. And their work was carried on in the open, even as this socialist meeting is being conducted, with the press on hand, with all the visitors that wanted to come, the hall packed with the strikers themselves. And when this committee finally reduced itself to ten to make negotiations with the mill owners, it was agreed before they left that they must meet the mill owners alone.

No Counselors Needed

When they arrived in Boston they found that the mill owners had their lawyers on hand. The strikers objected to the presence of the lawyers. And Mr. Wood the great financier said, "Oh, we must have our counsel, we must have our attorneys." "Why?" one of the strikers said, "Don't you think that you can take care of your end of it as well as we can of ours? If you insist on having your lawyer, Congressman Henry, why we will have to send down to Lawrence and bring up our advisor Haywood." They finally concluded that they could get along without counselors on either side. Time and again we hear it said that the workers can't do this business for themselves; that they haven't the education, they haven't the intelligence. And now remember that those Lawrence strikers were on the very lowest stratum. They were receiving wages so low that there were none who had a job so mean that he would leave it to come and scab in Lawrence. They were the people who were said to be the scum of Europe. But they could conduct their own business. And they conducted it successfully.

You will remember now that when the strike was declared, it was to prevent a reduction of wages of 30 cents. When the strike was organized the strikers demanded the reduction of hours, a reinstatement of the 30 cents, and a general increase of 15 percent. In the course of negotiations the adjustment was finally made on the basis of five percent for the highest paid, and 25 percent for the lowest paid (applause), those who needed it most; time and a quarter for overtime; readjustment of the premium system, and no discrimination against any man or woman or kid for the part that they took in the strike. You know, at the time of the great anthracite strike of 1902, John Mitchell, the "greatest labor leader that the world has ever known" (laughter) said that in all great battles there are some soldiers that must fall. That is, he said, in effect, that there can be a limited blacklist established. But the Lawrence strikers, the "ignorant workers," said, "We will have no fallen soldiers; not in this battle." Out of their own wisdom they said there would be no blacklist. And there was no blacklist.

No Race Prejudice Tolerated

There was a great and wonderful organization, an organization where we saw the Italian coming to the Turk notwithstanding that the war was going on in Tripoli, and inviting him to come up to his kitchen for soup. (Applause). You could see the German reaching across a mulligan stew shaking hands with a Frenchman. No question of nationality. I have spoken to those Italians in a meeting and asked them what country they belonged to. And they said, "The Industrial Workers of the World. " (Applause).

Nor did that limit their perception. When they saw the power that they had, they realized the necessity of controlling the city in which they lived. And after the strike we find the Socialist Party growing by the hundreds every meeting night. You say the workers can't conduct their own affairs. Let me tell you that in that strike all the money was handled by the strikers. The books were not well kept; there will be some questions perhaps as to the disbursement of the funds, and the manner in which they were receipted for. But just remember this; that when we grow a little bigger we are not going to run a revolution with a set of books. My advice to the workers there at the time the injunction was issued was to burn the books. (Applause). If it had not been for the fact that a financial report had been asked for, we would have burned the books.

Democracy Of The Strike

Get used to the manner in which a revolutionary strike is conducted. Figure in your own minds as to what it is going to amount to. Remember, there were as many as 50,000 people, men, women and children on relief during the latter part of that strike, and something less than $80,000 to take care of them for ten weeks. So they handled the finances well. They handled their strike committee well.

When the report came from the mill owners that the concessions were granted, the ten members of the committee brought it to the 112 members. The 112 members carried it out to the different nationalities, where it was voted upon. And when the different nationalities accepted it they met on the Common. Now remember, the town hall meetings in New England states are lawful. Their action is legal. But we didn't have a town hall big enough to hold 27,000. So they met under the vaulted blue tabernacle, on the Common. Do you question whether this organization believes in political action or not? There on the Common the proposition was submitted to the strikers. And I saw men, women and children vote for an increase in wages, for a reduction of hours, for better shop conditions. And that is political action. Every mass action of the working class against the capitalist class is a political action.

Significance Of The Impending Trial

And now we are here asking you tonight for more of that kind of action. I wish it were possible for the workers of this country to realize the tremendous significance of the impending trial in Lawrence. If you could realize that any one of you who addresses a handful of men might at some future time following the speech that you make, be sent to jail and tried for murder or any crime that comes out of it. No matter even though you had only said the Lord's prayer at the meeting—the fact that you had addressed a gathering and some crime was perpetrated over which you had no control and which, if you had known about, you would have done anything to prevent—that is the condition you are confronting. Now, there is a manner in which the lives of these men can be saved. When the four cigarmakers in Tampa, Florida, were sent to jail the cigarmakers' union, 10,000 strong, went on a general strike demanding a writ of habeas corpus, and the second day of that strike the men were released from jail. When Durand, the secretary of the coal heavers' union in France, addressed a meeting at Rouen, two months later a man was killed. Durand was arrested and charged with murder as a result of his alleged incendiary speech sometime previous. The labor unions of France took up his cause and they threatened a general strike. The result was that the sentence was commuted. Instead of the guillotine he was given 12 years in prison. But the workers said, "No; if you can send Durand to prison for twelve years you can send any or all of us to prison. Either throw open the doors or put him to the guillotine." And they went on with their agitation for a general strike. And the result was that the doors of the prison were thrown open and Durand stepped forth a free man.

Here you have the same power. It is going to require all the power you have got. You will have to work harder for Ettor and Giovannitti than you worked even for Moyer, Haywood and Pettibone. The capitalist class are feeling our strength. They see the tremendous growth of socialism; they are going to stop that growth if they possibly can. They are going to stop the growth of unionism. It will require your every effort. And let me appeal to you tonight, comrades, one and all to stand shoulder to shoulder, hand in hand, heart to heart and mind to mind, and you can do for Ettor and Giovannitti even as you did for me. (Tremendous applause).

CPSIA information can be obtained
at www.ICGtesting.com
Printed in the USA
BVOW06s1940270817
493094BV00015B/122/P

9 781610 010108